D0979851

# 20
## CONTROVERSIES
## THAT ALMOST
## KILLED A
## CHURCH

# 20

# CONTROVERSIES
## THAT ALMOST
# KILLED A
# CHURCH

**Paul's Counsel to the Corinthians**
### and the Church Today

# RICHARD L. GANZ

PUBLISHING
P.O. BOX 817 • PHILLIPSBURG • NEW JERSEY 08865-0817

© 2003 by Richard L. Ganz

All rights reserved. No part of this book may be reproduced, stored in a retrieval system, or transmitted in any form or by any means—electronic, mechanical, photocopy, recording, or otherwise—except for brief quotations for the purpose of review or comment, without the prior permission of the publisher, P&R Publishing Company, P.O. Box 817, Phillipsburg, New Jersey 08865-0817.

Scripture quotations are from the HOLY BIBLE, NEW INTERNATIONAL VERSION®. NIV®. Copyright © 1973, 1978, 1984 by International Bible Society. Used by permission of Zondervan Publishing House. All rights reserved.

Italics within Scripture quotations indicate emphasis added.

*Page design by UDG Designworks*
*Typesetting by Michelle Feaster*

Printed in the United States of America

Library of Congress Cataloging-in-Publication Data

Ganz, Richard L.
    Twenty controversies that almost killed a church : Paul's counsel to the Corinthians and the church today / Richard L. Ganz.
        p.   cm.
    Includes index.
    ISBN 0-87552-790-6
    1. Bible. N.T. Corinthians, 1st—Criticism, interpretation, etc.
I. Title.

BS2675.52.G36 2003
227'.206—dc21

                                        2003047119

To the congregation and elders (Aubrey Ayer, Iain Campbell, Alaisdar Graham) of the Ottawa Reformed Presbyterian Church, where I have had the pleasure and privilege of serving for twenty-three years. May our sovereign Lord grant us many more fruitful years together! (1Cor. 1:4–9)

# CONTENTS

# ACKNOWLEDGMENTS

I would like to thank Allan Fisher and his staff at P&R Publishing for being willing to publish a book that addresses controversial issues in the church. It is only natural to want to shy away from controversy. It is courageous to be willing to face them. So once again, thank you.

I would especially like to thank Sharlene Mekonnen for her outstanding and painstaking editorial work. I can hear her now saying as she worked on this, "The issues are sharp enough. Let's put it in a 'kindler, gentler' tone."

This book is intended to help you live more fully and faithfully for God at a time when living faithfully is increasingly difficult. The pressures against godly living have escalated, and struggles abound on every side. That is why 1 Corinthians is such an ideal text for us to study.

Should we think that the Corinthians were different from us? They faced pressures. They encountered snares. They experienced trials of all kinds, like we do. It is easy to see only the sin in the Corinthian church. But Paul, when he wrote this letter to them, saw them as a holy people waiting upon God (1 Cor. 1:2). He also referred to them as "saints." In the midst of some of our most difficult times, God continues to see us as his people. What an encouragement!

Paul opened his letter by pronouncing "grace and peace" upon the church (1 Cor. 1:3). These are blessings that come from God. He then expressed that he loved them so much that he "always thank[ed] God" for them (v. 4). Regardless of the weaknesses in their lives, he reminded them that as believers they were "enriched in every way" (v. 5). They possessed every spiritual gift that enabled them to wait for the coming of Christ patiently and to face temptation righteously. He gave them a great promise: "God will keep you strong to the end, so that you will be blameless on the day of our Lord Jesus Christ" (v. 8). They did not have to depend on their own strength because "God . . . is faithful" (v. 9). It is our faithful God who helps us face every problem that comes our way, so that we will be a holy people.

It is important to remember these encouragements, because immediately after expressing them, Paul tackled some of the serious issues that were threatening the church. We can thank God for those issues that brought such challenges to the Corinthian believers. From a distance of two thousand years, we are able to see the snares that we must avoid in the Christian life and the goal of godliness that we must pursue. It is my hope that we will learn strategies that enable us to walk righteously in the midst of an evil and despairing generation.

*Discussion questions are available in the back of this book, beginning on page 245.*

O ur church is blessed with leaders who are strong-minded. Every elder has definite views on individual issues, but it is a kind providence that we always arrive at agreement. In fact, in all the years we have worked together, I can't remember a single battle over the numerous difficult issues we face. What is the means God uses to accomplish this unity? Each of us is committed to something far beyond a personal agenda. We are first of all committed to the advance of the kingdom of Christ and his church. We really listen to each other and entertain ideas that may be very different from our own. Also, and most importantly, we are committed to a biblical resolution to each problem we face in the church. This immediately reduces the number of possible solutions.

This is not the case in every church. In my wider experience with church life, and perhaps in your experience as well, some church leaders are unable to reach agreement. They compete with each other, try to promote their own agendas,

> ### *1 CORINTHIANS 1:10–17*
>
> [10]I appeal to you, brothers, in the name of our Lord Jesus Christ, that all of you agree with one another so that there may be no divisions among you and that you may be perfectly united in mind and thought. [11]My brothers, some from Chloe's household have informed me that there are quarrels among you. [12]What I mean is this: One of you says, "I follow Paul"; another, "I follow Apollos"; another, "I follow Cephas"; still another, "I follow Christ."

and have their own group of followers. There are power struggles and lack of respect for God's providential placement of co-workers in leadership. Some of these churches have forced pastor after pastor from his position of leadership. This is an abysmal example to the body of Christ that they are leading and does not yield the blessing of God.

There is to be complete agreement, not only among the officers of the church but also in the entire church. Paul said, "All of you agree with one another so that there may be no divisions among you and that you be perfectly united in mind and thought" (1 Cor. 1:10). Think of it—no divisions in the body. A division of one's physical body is a horrible thought. A divided church is just as gruesome! Perfect unity is something we all greatly value, in our physical bodies and in the church body.

The situation of the Corinthian church was anything but unity. In fact, this is the first issue that Paul addressed after he greeted the church and expressed his thanks for them. Throughout his letter he came back again and again to the is-

> [13]Is Christ divided? Was Paul crucified for you? Were you baptized into the name of Paul? [14]I am thankful that I did not baptize any of you except Crispus and Gaius, [15]so no one can say that you were baptized into my name. [16](Yes, I also baptized the household of Stephanas; beyond that, I don't remember if I baptized anyone else.) [17]For Christ did not send me to baptize, but to preach the gospel—not with words of human wisdom, lest the cross of Christ be emptied of its power.

sue of unity. Every other problem in the church was influenced by the lack of unity and could not be effectively solved as long as the church was divided.

Paul got to the heart of the issue. He reminded the Corinthians that they possessed every spiritual blessing in Jesus Christ so they were able to live holy lives. The point he wanted to make is that holiness and disputes and divisions stand in opposition to each other. A church is not holy and quarrelsome at the same time. The apostle was not naive. He knew that as long as people are alive there would be conflicts and divisions. But he knew that it is horrible to see it happen and that it should be avoided if at all possible. As Paul said in Romans, "If it is possible, as far as it depends on you, live at peace with everyone" (Rom. 12:18).

The immediate question comes to mind, "Why then do such quarrels arise?" This is the same issue James raised in his epistle. It is a question he answered this way, "Fights and quarrels . . . come from your desires that battle within you. You want something but don't get it. You kill and covet, but you cannot have what you want. You quarrel and fight. You do not have, because you do not ask God. When you ask, you do not receive, because you do not ask God. When you ask, you do not receive, because you ask with wrong motives, so that you may spend what you get on your pleasures" (James 4:1–3). James's answer is revealing. Fights and quarrels break out because people are self-oriented, self-directed, self-serving, self-interested, self-consumed, and self-obsessed. They always want more for themselves. Selfishness is at the heart of the fighting and quarreling in the church.

However, James did not stop at the analysis of the problem. He also gave a solution, "Ask God." We should ask God in the right way, with the right motives, not so that we can gratify our desires but so that we can help others. I remember hearing Dr. James Kennedy, pastor of Coral Ridge Presbyterian Church, speak on a related issue. He said that in twenty-five years of pastoral ministry he had never prayed for something that would advance himself. While the church community has learned from the world that self is most important, Dr. Kennedy presented a different model. Maybe that is why his church has weathered the numerous storms that have destroyed so many other churches.

Consider every case where there is quarreling and fighting. Aren't selfishness and selfish ambition involved? The apostle Paul said that quarrels are schismatic. This means that quarrels rip or tear apart. These quarrels rip up and tear apart the body of Christ. The result is that the church, rather than being unified, has a group here and a group there. Each group is alienated from the other. According to Chloe, a central figure in the Corinthian church, groups fought and disputed with each other over allegiance to Paul, Peter, Apollos, or Christ. Can

Christ be made to compete against his servants in some kind of personality contest?

Over the years, I have mediated in several church battles. These battles are ugly events born of pride and selfishness. One of the things I have found is that the perpetrators are never concerned for the church. They are concerned for their desires, interests, or ambition, just as Paul said.

One of the forms of selfishness expressed by the Corinthians was the desire to raise their standing in the eyes of others by being associated with someone important. There is a certain security in being part of a clique. But in 1 Corinthians 1:18–31, Paul reminded them of how differently we as Christians should approach life—with humility. The fact that God chose the weak, lowly, and despised should give us comfort. We're *in*, and we don't have to worry about losing that because of how ordinary we are.

Paul also said, "be perfectly joined together" or "be perfectly united," using language that makes us think that he was talking about marriage. But he was not; he was referring to the church. It is inevitable that communities, even Christian communities, will at times be torn apart. The crucial issue is whether we will work to bring about mending. We are aware of how important this is in the physical body. The divided parts of the body must be brought together in unity, so that mending can take place.

In Matthew 4:21, the fishermen James and John were in a boat with their father, mending their nets. The Greek verb *katartizō* is used for the word *mend*. This mending process had to be done regularly to make sure they didn't lose their livelihood by losing fish! Relationships have gaps like holes in a net. We must always look out for these holes and be ready to mend them. All of us must at the least show sympathy to the hurting, the suffering, the "torn-apart" people all around us. We must let their situations affect us! We must look beyond our troubles to help others. Problems won't necessarily disappear just because we become involved. But at the same time, the mending process is greatly facilitated when people realize that others care and want to help. Mending can start from something as seemingly insignificant as that.[1]

For members of the church to be united, there must be mending of all the hurts and sins that have occurred. This uniting and mending must be a complete process, because the text continues to urge the Corinthians to be of the same mind. Which mind is this? In Philippians 2 we learn that it is the mind of Christ, a mind that is marked by humility and obedience, even unto death. This mindset will not dishonor God by fighting, bickering, and self-righteously killing the church. This is the antidote to divisive quarreling.

We also are to have the same judgment, that is, what we believe should correspond with what others in the church believe. I remember an unbeliever who tried to join my congregation. Doctrine after doctrine got in the way, and eventually he left. But we who stay together are to be of one mind and one judgment regarding our faith in Jesus Christ. Some of the lesser issues may see us diverge, but in the heart of the matter, our judgments correspond. This is why the model of the teachers of the church is so important. These leaders form the thinking of the congregation. If the teaching of the leaders is sound and united, the congregation will grow strong and united—and for this they should be grateful.

---

1. For more on this, see Richard L. Ganz, *Psychobabble* (Wheaton, Ill.: Crossway, 1993), 91–99.

Throughout the history of the church, unity was the clear intention. When the Judaizers demanded the circumcision of the Gentiles, elders from all the churches met in the first synod[2] to resolve the issue. After they reached their conclusion, a letter expressing their resolution was circulated to all the churches. It was expected that they would all agree. In fact, that is what Presbyterian church government is all about. When the elders come to biblically based agreement on an issue, the entire church should put its quarrels aside and be of one mind and judgment. Even if the elders' decision must be challenged, it is never to be done in a divisive manner. The dispute should then be resolved by the presbytery.[3] Presbytery should be called to adjudicate only when the lower court[4] finds itself unable to resolve the issue successfully. A church problem should not be decided privately. It certainly should never be decided by gossip or slander.

Paul's point was simple. If oneness of mind and judgment marks the church, it is because Christ is one. Oneness is a basic principle of the Christian church, and that principle should affect our attitude about the church. So often, though, the church is run down most by the people who should be building it up.

Many times, believers who are critical are in churches with a good doctrinal position, a good minister, and good elders. Yet the people grumble and complain, and no one stops them. I spoke on the subject of the resurrection of Christ at a con-

2. A synod is a joint meeting of the elders of all the churches.

3. Presbytery is made up of elders of all the churches in a particular geographic region.

4. Elders of a particular congregation are the lower court.

ference, and a person said to me, "Dr. Ganz, that was wonderful. Our pastor has never preached on the resurrection." I was not flattered. I knew the man whom this person was criticizing to be a sound, biblical pastor in an orthodox denomination. I had heard him preach and had been blessed. I couldn't imagine that he had never preached on the resurrection, so I knew I was dealing with someone who was sowing discord. I asked the pastor if he had ever preached on that topic, and he produced for me his recent series on the resurrection. I then returned to this man who had been complaining. I told him that what he had said about his pastor's teaching was false and that he must stop speaking against a godly ministry at once, or discipline would follow.

There are also people who consciously build the church of God by building up his people. They are not always very noticeable. Simple acts of kindness and encouragement, and wise words of advice or rebuke, are deeds of love that are sometimes inconspicuous. Believers who devote themselves to others can be assured that they will never be unnoticed by God, because the Scripture says, "Anyone [who] . . . gives even a cup of cold water to one of these little ones . . . he will certainly not lose his reward" (Matt. 10:42).

The life of the church is up to *the church*. When we are in a church that keeps us safe from the storms of heresy and compromise swirling about us, we should be thankful. I once counseled a family whose oldest son sat across from me with his lip curled in what seemed to be a permanent sneer. He complained about everything and everyone, but especially his parents. One day he returned to see me, shaking and weeping. In a state of shock, he said, "They told me to leave—how can they do that?" What did he expect? That he could freely complain and provoke vicious quarrels? When he belittled his parents and everything they gave to him and did for him, did he expect to receive hugs and kisses in return? His behavior was serious business, and it cost him his home and family.

Church members as well should realize that persistent divisive grumbling and complaining can cost them their church family. Paul put it this way in Romans 16:17, "Watch out for those who cause divisions and put obstacles in your way that are contrary to the teaching you have learned. *Keep away from them.*" Notice that it says of them, "Such people are not serving Christ, but their own appetites." In other words, these individuals who tear up churches and who teach doctrines contrary to what they learned are selfish, self-centered, self-indulgent individuals with whom believers are to have no fellowship. Unity in Christ doesn't mean that you have Christian fellowship with everyone, but only those who are biblical. In this instance it means that fellowship and unity cannot include divisions in the body.

To accomplish this, Philippians 2:2 advises us to be "like-minded . . . being one in spirit and purpose." The next verse adds, "Do nothing out of selfish ambition or vain conceit." Once again we are warned against selfishness and pride. Expanding on this, the apostle says, "In humility consider others better than yourselves. Each of you should look not only to your own interests, but also to the interests of others." Such behavior will defeat selfish divisiveness every time.

**C**an you remember the time you first believed the gospel? I can. Never before in my life, and never since, did anything have the impact that the gospel had on me! It thoroughly overpowered me. It was beyond any reality I had ever imagined. In fact, I experienced it as dying. The force of the gospel broke in upon me, leaving me feeling as if my very life were being taken away. My old life *was* being taken away. Things would never again be the same with my family, my profession, and my personal life. At the same time, there was an underlying sense of peace and safety in my soul that had never been there before.

I felt compelled to immediately tell people about what I had experienced, and I assumed that all people I spoke to would have the same response I had. But they didn't. At times people listened politely. On some occasions they argued with me. At other times they didn't listen. Only rarely did anyone who listened to my story believe the gospel.

This was discouraging. I wondered, *"How can they dispute*

**1 CORINTHIANS 1:18–21**

¹⁸For the message of the cross is foolishness to those who are perishing, but to us who are being saved it is the power of God. ¹⁹For it is written:

> I will destroy the wisdom of the wise;
>> the intelligence of the intelligent I will frustrate.

²⁰Where is the wise man? Where is the scholar? Where is the philosopher of this age? Has not God made foolish the wisdom of the world? ²¹For since in the wisdom of God the world through its wisdom did not know him, God was pleased through the foolishness of what was preached to save those who believe.

*what seems so incontrovertible to me?"* *"How can they turn away?"* But they did. What's more, sometimes they hated me for what I had said to them as it became clear that I was not saying, "This is a nice option for you," but rather, "If you don't believe this, you will be judged and damned forever."

It was also confusing. When I practiced as a psychologist I believed nothing, yet people listened and did what I told them to do. Now, as a Christian, I was convinced of the truth, but people didn't seem to care. I wasn't able to explain this seeming contradiction until I understood the passage we are examining: "The message of the cross is foolishness to those who are perishing, but to us who are being saved it is the power of God."

A simple truth became real to me. My experience was not odd; it is common to believers. It is consistent with the Scriptures. We are not dealing with psychology or philosophy, disciplines that can be accommodated to fit human speculation and reason, likes and dislikes. We are dealing with the only message that can bring salvation to a person's life, and we shouldn't be surprised at either the variety or intensity of responses. That's the point of this passage. The preaching of the cross is foolishness to those who are perishing *and* the power of God to those who believe.

The question, though, is this: Why is the preaching of the cross foolishness to those who are perishing?

Consider for a moment the Lord Jesus Christ. His life was filled with humility. He did not aspire to greatness, and he gave up all the prerogatives of earthly greatness. He came into the world through the womb of a poor, young Jewish virgin. His birth was in the most humble location, a manger in a stable. He didn't use his miracles to procure wealth, or even a following. Indeed at every point, when it seemed he had made it, he said something that riled his public. For example, after he fed the thousands, they wanted to make him king. But he told them that they should trust in him *for eternal life*. We read, "From this time many of his disciples turned back and no longer followed him" (John 6:66).

Toward the end of his life, when the men brought Jesus before their rulers, it was not so they could learn wisdom from him. Instead it was to curse him, rip off his garments and bloody his back with a steel-tipped whip, pluck his beard, and pierce his hands and feet. He was viewed with contempt then, and he is viewed with contempt now. Why should this be a surprise? Why should the world suddenly identify with a Jewish carpenter whose words and deeds brought him a violent death?

In these eight verses in 1 Corinthians 1 (vv. 18–25) the

word *foolishness* is used five times. If you translate the word *fool* from Greek to English you have the word *moron.* To speak of salvation from death and hell through the suffering and death of Christ is moronic to the world.

What do the world's philosophies teach? The philosophy of the world is summed up by the Humanist Society, which claims that we must save ourselves. This is why the preaching of the cross is moronic to the world. The world teaches that we must save ourselves; the Bible teaches that we can be saved only through the work of Jesus Christ.

The apostle Paul was brilliant, not only as a theologian but also as a philosopher. He read the philosophers and poets and quoted them in his discussions, such as in Acts 17. But when it came to preaching the gospel, he said, "I resolved to know nothing while I was with you except Jesus Christ and him crucified" (1 Cor. 2:2). What he meant was that he would give himself over to no one but Christ and to no philosophy but the cross.

When Malcolm Muggeridge, one of England's leading intellects, became a Christian, a letter to the editor in a large newspaper spoke derisively of him. This article declared that Muggeridge "found Jesus at the same time he was losing his marbles." What was this writer saying? He was declaring that when Muggeridge became a Christian, he became a fool. Paul said, "We are fools for Christ's sake" (1 Cor. 4:10). He recognized that there would be no approval from the world.

Men don't want to hear Jesus say, "I am the light of the world." Men hate "I am the way, the truth, and the life" and detest hearing "no one comes to the Father except through me." Why should they hate this? Because these statements declare that there is truth—not truth as you like it or want it, but absolute truth. This truth announces one way and one God!

If you take a course in philosophy at almost any university, you will hear, "The only absolute is that there are no absolutes." To the world, those who are perishing, the gospel of one God and one way is foolishness. They applaud the words of the astronaut who said, "I have looked into the heavens, and there is no God." In the minds of unbelievers, an empirical test has been done and everyone can rest, because there is no God. But God said, "Although they claimed to be wise, they became fools" (Rom. 1:22). Even the children's catechism has the question, "Can you see God?" The answer is, "I cannot see God, but he always sees me."

Modern people put their hope in evolution. That is, they put hope in chance. They believe in nothing, because chance is nothing. It doesn't exist. The philosopher and theologian Dr. Francis Schaeffer spoke strongly against evolution because he realized that the only two worldviews facing humanity are creation or evolution. People are either the handiwork of a personal loving Creator God or the product of chance. That is, they are meaningless, their world is meaningless, and their existence is hopeless.

Why is the preaching of the cross so dramatic for believers and unbelievers? The text says it is "foolishness" or "moronic" to those who are perishing, and it is the power of God to those who are being saved. This description gives us a clue as it reveals the two conditions of humankind—those who are perishing (the lost) and those who are being saved. There are only two alternatives for the race. A person is saved by the grace of God, through the preaching of the Word of God. Or a person is utterly lost and destroyed forever in hell. The horror for the lost is that those who are perishing do not come to the preaching, the one source that could extricate them from their awful plight, but instead they despise and loathe it.

I remember preaching in Hyde Park in London. One section of the park is a gathering place for a heterogeneous mix of people who come to hear impromptu speeches. The crowd paid no attention to the person who had been speaking before me. I began by asking a question of the almost nonexistent crowd: "What is a Jew like me, from New York City, doing here, telling you about Jesus Christ?" A Muslim fundamentalist heard me say that and ran over, shouting at the top of his lungs, "This man is Satan! This man is Satan!" This had the effect of attracting a great many more people. Within a short time, a crowd of people was listening to me preach Christ. This Muslim and a group of his friends surrounded me as I spoke, but in spite of the intimidation, their hatred of the gospel gave me the opportunity to preach to many, many lost souls. In that crowd, many hearts were touched. By the end of my message, numerous people were either deeply convicted of their sin or screaming at me. There were women, whom I would assume have never yelled at someone in public before, screaming at me. One Muslim woman was calling me the worst thing she could think of: "He is John Wayne. He is John Wayne!"

What happened? It's simple. The preaching of the cross was foolish, moronic, and repulsive to many there who were on their way to hell. Their loathing of God was incited and intensified by the preaching. But for those who were being saved, it was God's power and thus able to break into their hearts and turn them to Christ.

That message was dynamite from heaven—it was explosive! That is what all preaching of the cross is meant to be. It is not meant to be a sweet little homily during which everyone nods in agreement or just plain nods off! It is God's power, because the preaching of the cross says, "Your salvation, your deliverance, is by the work of another. It is not of yourself. It is not by your own strength." A world committed to the theology of "save yourself" can only find such preaching intolerable.

The true preaching of the Word has always brought controversy, but it remains the absolute, foundational reality for all who are being saved. It reminds us of several important lessons for the people of God.

It helps us to see where we stand. Many churches in our society want to know only a little bit about Jesus and a great deal about psychology. Recently I was asked to speak at an influential church in a large city. I chose the subject "The Sufficiency of Scriptures in Counseling" and was told to choose another topic because that was too controversial. Should a view of *sola scriptura* be controversial? Should the conclusions about the heart of humankind reached by secular philosophers such as Freud, Jung, and others be preferred over what the Scripture teaches us about the heart of people? In seminaries too, people have chosen to study those philosophers of human understanding rather than search the Scriptures for wisdom to counsel people. Yet Scripture gives the supreme insight about how to understand the way people are created by God and to tell them what he expects of them. It is incumbent on Christians who have the particular gift of understanding people to study the human heart and behavior in the light of Scripture and to direct people in the ways of God.

Several years ago I was asked to do a televised pro-life debate. The format was sure to make the pro-life participant look foolish, since the culture was so blatantly anti-Christian. Because I believed this debate was something I should do as part of my Christian witness, I did not care if I looked foolish. I knew that if I were being faithful to my Lord, I could not look anything but foolish *to those that are perishing*. My concern was that I glorify Christ. I had in mind the approval of my Lord on that last day, "Well done, you good and faithful servant." At some point, his servants have to settle the issue of whether they are prepared to be fools for Christ or will settle for being respected and approved by the world.

The preaching of the cross also helps us to see where others stand. As long as we are noncommittal, the people around us are free to be the same. But when we become faithful and preach the message of the cross, the demand of a holy God that all people everywhere repent of their sin and unbelief (Acts 17:30), then we learn a great deal about others. Some who we thought were our friends turn away from us. They don't want to identify with a "fanatic." We experience what it means to bear "the disgrace he [Christ] bore" (Heb. 13:13). We see how easily and quickly people assess us as foolish.

The preaching of the Word helps us to see where human wisdom stands. In this passage Paul quoted from Isaiah 29:14, "I will destroy the wisdom of the wise; the intelligence of the intelligent I will frustrate." He stated clearly that the wisdom of people will be destroyed. All wisdom that arrays itself against God, all that pompously declares that the preaching of the cross is foolish, will itself be proven foolish when God destroys it.

The verse Paul quoted had a tremendous historical context for God's people. Sennacherib, king of Assyria, was planning to destroy Judah. He sent his field commander, backed by a large army, to Jerusalem to mock the Israelites and their God. He reminded them that the gods of other nations had not been able to save them from destruction by the mighty Sennacherib. When this terrifying situation was brought before the prophet Isaiah, the Lord responded with these comforting words, "Do not be afraid of what you have heard—those words with which the underlings of the king of Assyria have blasphemed me" (Isa. 37:5). In the dead of night, the angel of the Lord put to death 185,000 men in the Assyrian camp. When the soldiers got up the next morning—there were all the dead bodies! So Sennacherib, king of Assyria, broke camp and withdrew (Isa. 37:36–37).

Human wisdom avails nothing in the day of the Lord. All human might and power will come to naught as the Lord destroys the foolish. As we look at North America, sitting proud and pompous, making one pronouncement after another that ridicules, mocks, and slanders the Word of God, it is only a matter of time before it too is decisively judged if it will not repent. For there is no favored nation status with God, not even for the United States or Canada.

The preaching of the gospel helps us to see where God's wisdom stands. In 1 Corinthians 1:21 we read these simple, yet startling words, "For since in the wisdom of God the world through its wisdom did not know him." We see that God's wisdom makes him inscrutable to all those who rebel against him. People can know how the genetic code works and learn how to cure all manner of illnesses, but without a humble and contrite heart, people can never know God. Many times people do not want to know him, because they seek a god who would give them what they want, not a living and holy God of heaven and earth. That knowledge of God, ultimately, is all that matters. "Now this is eternal life: that they may know you, the only true God, and Jesus Christ, whom you have sent" (John 17:3). Humankind can never come to know God by philosophy or scholarship or debate. Man must recognize first his desperate need of salvation from sin, and only then will God reveal himself to fallen humankind. He will not be revealed as the man upstairs, a figure on a medallion, or the good-luck charm we invoke when we fall on bad times. He is the holy God of heaven.

God does not intend for you to work out your salvation in your own strength and wisdom. God's way is simply and eloquently expressed in this passage, "God was pleased through the foolishness of what was preached to save those who believe" (1 Cor. 1:21). This passage is a confrontation with human wisdom. It is a concord of your desperate need and God's gracious supply. It is a consideration of the salvation of the holy God of heaven, because the suffering Savior died for our sins. The Jews could not even look on this. The Gentiles have been no better. Paul desires that all his readers and hearers listen to the Word of God and not reject Christ. He longs for them not to hope in human wisdom but believe in Jesus Christ and be saved.

**G**od mercifully removes some individuals from lifestyles of deep sin that could only have led to death and puts them on the road to life. It is sad when they become harsh, severe, and judgmental of others over minor points of the law.

There was a man who worshiped in our congregation years ago. He had been a drug abuser and had spent time in jail. After I spoke to him about the Lord, he made a profession of faith. But almost immediately he proceeded to involve himself in trivial controversy with everyone in the congregation. I used to marvel at his arrogance and mean-spiritedness. It was a relief when he left the church. Unfortunately, he went on to trouble other churches. In the ten years after he left the church, I continued to receive calls from people asking me how to deal with this man. This is an example of the behavior that concerned Paul in 1 Corinthians 1:26–31. People in Corinth had come to faith in Christ, but instead of remembering who they had been, they became the chief critics and troublemakers in the church.

### 1 CORINTHIANS 1:26–31

²⁶Brothers, think of what you were when you were called. Not many of you were wise by human standards; not many were influential; not many were of noble birth. ²⁷But God chose the foolish things of the world to shame the wise; God chose the weak things of the world to shame the strong. ²⁸He chose the lowly things of this world and the despised things—and the things that are not—to nullify the things that are, ²⁹so that no one may boast before him. ³⁰It is because of him that you are in Christ Jesus, who has become for us wisdom from God—that is, our righteousness, holiness and redemption. ³¹Therefore, as it is written: "Let him who boasts boast in the Lord."

How did Paul respond to this? He said, "Brothers, think of what you were when you were called." This was Paul's antidote to the boastful pride and arrogance that is such a besetting sin in the lives of many people. Remembering helps us to have compassion, whether for an unbeliever needing Christ or for brothers and sisters in the faith. We may think that other people do not understand the Christian life as well as we do, but we may be surprised one day to realize that they have a deeper level of understanding!

Paul reminded the Corinthians that they were "not wise by human standards" and were "not influential." The church often acts as if God's plans will be thwarted if its members aren't sponsored by some powerful figure. We become secularists in this regard. We behave as if the power of the world's mighty individuals is greater than the prayers of God's humble saints.

"Not many were of noble birth," Paul wrote. The inscriptions on the catacombs, where early Roman believers hid from persecution, showed that the church was constituted of the lower classes of society. The philosopher Celsus wrote toward the end of the second century that Christians "are the most vulgar, the most uneducated of persons. They are like frogs holding a symposium around a swamp, or worms convening in mud." This Christian faith, which vanquished kingdoms over the centuries, was an army of the inconsequential.

You are *called*. Because of God's gracious work, you have a new heart and a new life. In a formal debate that I had with members of a psychology department, my goal was to demonstrate the value of the Scriptures in counseling. The perspective of the chairman of the psychology department was, "If you counsel from the Bible, your ideas are not even worth considering alongside our psychological theorists." This was a Christian college!

The Scriptures direct us to a manner of life befitting our calling as new people in Christ. In Ephesians 4:1 we read, "Live a life worthy of the calling you have received." Then it describes that calling—a life of humility, gentleness, patience, forbearance, unity, and peace. This new life is opposed to the arrogance, pride, and meanness of the world around us. The only way the world can interpret this is to conclude that we are nothing.

"God did not call us to be impure, but to live a holy life," Paul wrote in 1 Thessalonians 4:7. Our lives are changed to become holy. The same idea was restated in 2 Timothy 1:9, "[God] has saved and called us to a holy life." As a new creation of God, you are to "be holy in all you do; for it is written, 'Be holy, because I am holy'" (1 Peter 1:16). God called us out of sin and darkness so that we might declare his praise. This only makes sense, because of the great riches and mercy we have received from God.

God shamed the wise and the strong. He reproached the "things that are" (1 Cor. 1:28). The world says that people are great when they are intelligent or beautiful, talented or wealthy. But God says that these characteristics count for nothing with him. If you are proud of your gifts, then God says you are *nothing*. He is no respecter of persons. He chooses whomever he pleases. It is important to get our priorities straight and see that the kingdom's view of greatness is antithetical to the world's view.

John the Baptist had no wealth, beautiful home, or aristocratic ancestry. Instead he lived in the desert, wore camel-hair clothing, and ate locusts and wild honey. When the daughter of King Herod's wife pleased the king with her dancing, Herod offered to give her whatever she wished. She talked to her mother, who wanted John killed so that he would stop preaching and making her feel guilty. The girl asked for the head of John the Baptist, and her wish was granted. No one stepped in to save him. Yet Jesus said that John was the greatest man in the world! God is not mocked. The world will be shocked one day to learn who are the great people in God's eyes. Though they have nothing of the world's frills, they possess a greatness that is from heaven.

This heavenly greatness points to God. No one can stand before God and say, "I achieved on my own." On the contrary, God chose those who have nothing to boast about themselves. There was nothing in us that merited God's favor. There was nothing in us that deserved God's mercy. There is no reason why he should choose us over others. All of salvation is for the glory of God alone. We know that we have been saved by grace alone through faith in Christ. As Paul said in 1 Corinthians 1:29, "No one may boast before [God]." If the church lived with this in its heart, many controversies would be rapidly silenced!

Take time to reflect on what you were when you were called. You may have come from a life of deep sin. You may have had a past of profound pride, or a good life that was empty without God. Your history may have been despairing and hopeless. Now you have Christ, but don't forget from where you have come. Take time to remember that not many of you were wise, influential, or noble. That is for a purpose— so that now, as a saved man or woman, you would remain humble. The word *humble* means "to break into tiny little pieces." Jesus called Moses "the most humble man on earth." Augustine, when asked what were the three most important virtues, replied, "Humility, humility, humility."

Humility is a blessing to the church because it produces *charity*. Rather than being like the harsh and judgmental individual mentioned at the outset of this chapter, you are to be charitable. When a situation of difficulty comes your way, don't look first to your interests, but seek to minister to others. "In humility consider others better than yourselves" (Phil. 2:3). Remember that "humility . . . comes from wisdom" (James 3:13), and that you must "clothe yourselves with humility" because "God opposes the proud but gives grace to the humble" (1 Peter 5:5). We are to "trust in the name of the LORD" (Ps. 20:7) and "on [your] bed . . . remember God" (Ps. 63:6). "In the night I remember your name, O LORD" (Ps. 119:55). "Remember . . .

the LORD your God" (Deut. 8:2; Neh. 4:14; 1 Sam. 14:11). "Remember your Creator in the days of your youth" (Eccles. 12:1). "Do this remembering me" (1 Cor. 11:24).

We remember names and dates for school tests. I have a friend, a family medicine physician, who remembers complete shows from *The Simpsons*. I know someone else who can repeat the dialogue from thirty-year-old Woody Allen movies. But do we remember who we were? Do we remember the God who saved us? "Remember God." Remember him now, while you still have the ability to remember. Remember him while your life can still make a difference. If you can't remember him, because you don't know him, then learn of him now. Learn of his great love, mercy, and grace. Learn of his sacrifice for sinners such as you and me. Flee to Christ and be saved from your sins. Spend the rest of your life not in quarreling, controversy, or despair but in remembering how great a God you have and how great a salvation he purchased for you. Remember that you were once dead in your sins, and now you are called to live a life worthy of a Christian. When you remember what God calls you to remember, you will never stumble or falter. Your life will be blessed, and the life of the church will be blessed as well.

**C**ontroversy hit the United Church of Canada when its moderator publicly denied the deity of Jesus Christ. Problems seem to be repeated throughout history by the church. At the beginning of his letter, Paul intimated that he was concerned about something more serious than church division. When one person followed Paul, another Peter, and another Christ (1 Cor. 1:12), the problem was no different from that of the United Church. It indicated that they didn't believe Jesus is God! They behaved as if he were just one leader among many. Therefore, with this erroneous thinking, members could choose whomever they wished to follow. The United Church moderator also said, "I don't believe Jesus was raised from the dead." The apostle Paul made it abundantly clear that true Christian faith hinges on the full acceptance of the teachings of Scripture. Thus, from the beginning of 1 Corinthians, where Christ's deity was denied, to the end of the book, where Christ's resurrection was denied, there were problems that could have destroyed the church in Corinth.

> **1 CORINTHIANS 1:30**
>
> ³⁰It is because of him that you are in Christ Jesus, who has become for us wisdom from God—that is, our righteousness, holiness and redemption.

Paul said, "If only for this life we have hope in Christ, we are to be pitied more than all men" (1 Cor. 15:19). In this verse, he countered individuals who reject Christ and deny him. He said in 1 Corinthians 1:30 that Jesus is everything. All that matters is Christ. Paul did not, in this brief statement, say that Christ is an aspect of the Christian life but rather that Christ is everything. He is our wisdom. He is our righteousness. He is our holiness. He is our redemption. Since our life is "in Christ," who is made to us wisdom, righteousness, holiness, and redemption, we are complete in him.

*Christ is our wisdom.* We live in a world where everyone wants wisdom, but wisdom is lacking. Because of this lack, we see the structures of our society falling apart. Our passage teaches that the wisdom of the world is completely foolish. But God has not left his people without wisdom. That would be impossible, for he is, as the text says, our wisdom. What does this mean?

Wisdom is first of all the fear of the Lord (Prov. 1:7). This wisdom is a gift from Christ. When we realized that we were weak, foolish, and hopelessly lost in sin, wisdom caused us to recognize that he found us and saved us in that condition. As believers in Jesus Christ, we are given the wisdom of the One who saved us. The Scriptures tell us that Jesus "learned obedience," and we must imitate him. We must continue to learn his wisdom by studying the commands of Scripture and *applying* them in our particular situations. We keep growing as we make use of the means he has given to us, the means of grace. Those means include the preaching of the Word, worship with other believers, prayer, and studying the Scriptures. As we imitate our Savior, who, "when they hurled their insults at him, he did not retaliate" (1 Peter 2:23), and who "entrusted himself to him [God] who judges justly" (1 Peter 2:23), we will be builders in God's kingdom.

*Christ is also our righteousness.* Most simply, the word *righteousness* means to be made right with God. Take note that the verse says, "He has become righteousness to us." It is not a righteousness of our own that we possess but the righteousness of Christ, which is why the Reformers called it an "alien righteousness." This is a hard thing for many people, because they hope in their own righteousness. The gospel strongly argues against that when it says that Christ's righteousness is counted to the one "who does not work but trusts in God who justifies the wicked." This "faith is credited as righteousness" (Rom. 4:5).

Another passage that presents this idea is 2 Corinthians 5:21, which states, "God made him who had no sin to be sin for us, so that in him we might become the righteousness of God." This has amazing significance for us sinners. It says, in effect, "Stop the worry. You are all right." If you belong to Jesus Christ you are not only forgiven and declared sinless. You are declared righteous. In fact, you are pronounced by God to possess the righteousness of Christ himself. When God looks at you, what he sees is Christ and Christ's righteousness alone. Can we absorb the significance of this? God's view of us who believe is that we have met all the demands of his holy justice. It is as if we lived perfectly just and righteous lives ourselves. That is what is meant when the Bible teaches that Christ became sin for us and we became righteousness in him. The whole idea is summed up in Philippians 3:9, where Paul teaches, "[We are] found in him, not having a righteousness of [our] own . . . but that which is through faith in Christ."

*Christ is also our sanctification.* The word *sanctification* means "to be made holy" or "to be made saints." Each believer is a saint in God's eyes! Someone who recently came to faith in Christ asked about saints during one of our discussions, "What is wrong with the Catholic church having a list of saints?" The real error isn't that it has saints, but it is the way that it decides who is a saint. God makes *all* his people saints when he brings them to a saving knowledge of himself. In addition to declaring them righteous, he is sanctifying his people—making them holy. When you are in union with Christ through faith, you are St. Steven, St. Anne, St. Robert, or St. Rebecca, because sainthood belongs to *all* the saints. The saints are the ones who are set apart from sin, set apart from impurity, and set apart for God and for the life in which they are made more and more holy. You are the set-apart people in whom God dwells. God is using your lives for his purposes to build his church.

*Christ is also our redemption.* He bought us back by paying the price that God demands, and that price is his life. It is his blood. You were under the power and mastery of sin. God said that sin had dominion over you, but he paid the price of sin's power. Peter wrote that the debt was paid "not with perishable things . . . but with the precious blood of Christ, a lamb without blemish" (1 Peter 1:18–19).

This passage in 1 Corinthians 1:30 teaches us that Jesus is everything to us. He doesn't just make it *possible* for us to be wise. He *is* wisdom to us. He doesn't just make it *possible* for us to be righteous. He *is* righteousness to us. He doesn't just make it *possible* for us to be sanctified. He *is* our sanctification. He is that set-apart One. He doesn't just make redemption possible. He *is* our redemption. This passage is saying what Paul said in Romans 11:36, "For from him and through him and to him are all things. To him be the glory forever. Amen." This text gloriously answers those who say Christ is not God. He is everything. He is the entirety of our redemption.

Because of this, we should possess an attitude of sheer humility and thanksgiving. We did absolutely nothing to receive that full redemption from God. We did nothing to be bought back from the curse of sin and death. We did nothing to set ourselves apart from the mass of humanity hurtling toward death and hell. Sinners saved by grace should be on their faces in thanks and adoration.

Paul had earlier said that the cross is foolishness to all who are perishing. We should place the highest value on the cross of Christ. The greatest emphasis in our lives should be on the suffering of Christ. Our fullest praise should be on the sufficiency of Christ. Our hope for eternal life is all "because of him" (1 Cor. 1:30). Those are beautiful words: "It is because of him." Whatever you hope as a Christian, it is because of him. Whatever you achieve in holiness, it is because of him. Whatever sin you are able to shed, it too is because of him. This text is all about him. He has become wisdom, righteousness, holiness, and redemption. This is the Savior. Behold him and rejoice. Behold him and praise. Behold him and be satisfied.

Who is Christ to you? When you sin, it is easy to despair of ever being what you desire to be in Christ. At those times let this text come to mind, telling you that it is not your striving or your seeking that will secure you in Christ. In spite of everything, you are secure. It is because of *him*. He has done it all. As difficult as it might be to believe at times, it is well with your soul because of him. What is Christ to you? He is to be everything! He is your wisdom, your righteousness, your sanctification, and your redemption. May you be able to say, "All that I am, I am in him. All that I hope for, I hope for through him."

In the opening section of 1 Corinthians 3, the deadly problem of divisions is addressed once again. These divisions were provoked by "jealousy and quarreling" (1 Cor. 3:3). Paul's indictment was, "You are still worldly." Though the Corinthians might have thought they sounded spiritual, because they said they followed Paul or Apollos (1 Cor. 3:4), their behavior was worldly, or carnal. The apostle did not esteem such behavior because he knew this mentality would only destroy the church. There are two particular sins that he addressed in this passage. The interesting thing about them is that they are not considered serious sins in the church. Yet Paul saw the spiritual danger that could tear the church apart. He wanted to stop it before it took hold.

What brings about divisive behavior in the church? We read in 1 Corinthians 3:1, "You are worldly." The word *worldly* is more literally translated "fleshly" or "carnal." Carnality is, most simply, our human nature in its weakness. This word is used ten times in the Bible. For example, in Romans

---

**1 CORINTHIANS 3:1-9**

¹Brothers, I could not address you as spiritual but as worldly—mere infants in Christ. ²I gave you milk, not solid food, for you were not yet ready for it. Indeed, you are still not ready. ³You are still worldly. For since there is jealousy and quarreling among you, are you not worldly? Are you not acting like mere men? ⁴For when one says, "I follow Paul," and another, "I follow Apollos," are you not mere men?

---

7:14 Paul commended the law saying, "The law is spiritual," but he said of himself, "I am unspiritual." In 2 Corinthians 1:12 he said that his holiness is with sincerity, not carnality, or worldliness. He was saying that sincerity is without any false motivations—it is for the benefit of the other and not oneself. Peter urged believers to abstain from carnal (worldly or fleshly) lusts in 1 Peter 2:11. These are lusts that enable people to accept the philosophies of the world. These philosophies change as the seasons change. Worldly persons accept them and practice them. They are in step with the world. In Romans 12:2 Paul said, "Do not conform any longer to the pattern of this world." In other words, "Don't be worldly." Rather, he said, "Be transformed by the renewing of your mind. Then you will be able to test and approve what God's will is—his good, pleasing, and perfect will." The worldly person, the carnal person, cannot do the will of God. He has to be transformed. His mind has to be changed. He must, in other words, be born again.

Paul was concerned about worldliness from the outset in

> ⁵What, after all, is Apollos? And what is Paul? Only servants, through whom you came to believe—as the Lord has assigned to each his task. ⁶I planted the seed, Apollos watered it, but God made it grow. ⁷So neither he who plants nor he who waters is anything, but only God, who makes things grow. ⁸The man who plants and the man who waters have one purpose, and each will be rewarded according to his own labor. ⁹For we are God's fellow workers; you are God's field, God's building.

his dealings with the Corinthians. In 1 Corinthians 1:18–25 he cautioned against imbibing the thinking and philosophical mindset of the culture around them. He was disturbed about them adopting an elitist mentality in 1 Corinthians 1:26–31. He warned against striving after worldly wisdom in 1 Corinthians 2. He summed up his concern about division in the churches as stemming from worldliness in 1 Corinthians 3. He fought against a carnality, a worldliness, that could divide and destroy the church. It was a carnality that manifested itself in Corinth in jealousy and quarreling.

The apostle Paul elaborated on the behavior that accompanied division—envy and quarreling (strife). It is a bit striking at first glance that these should be so prominent in Paul's concerns. They are not immorality, murder, or stealing. But they are mentioned along with other sins in Galatians 5:19–21 as "acts of the sinful nature." The word *flesh* that is employed in Galatians 5:19 is the same word used in our passage, which said that the Corinthians appeared carnal, or fleshly. They were still infants in relationship to Christ. This is a serious charge that Paul substantiates not by exposing some of their deeper sins but by pointing out their envy and strife. These behaviors in themselves were killing the church.

How powerful is envy? Envy can be on a small scale, such as it was in a childhood incident related by a friend. She said that when she was nine years old, she eagerly waited to open her Christmas present. On Christmas Eve, in her package was a doll—the gift she wanted! She anxiously watched her sister open her present. It was a doll, too! Her immediate thought was, "Why did Mom give her the best doll?" She quietly took her present upstairs to her bedroom, but her sister followed her. She came close and whispered in her ear, "*Do you want to trade dolls?*" In that instant she knew that her sister was envious of *her* doll! There are similar versions of envying each other's gifts played out by adults all the time.

When this word *envy* is used in the Bible, it is speaking about depraved and corrupt activity that is fueled by rage and hatred, such as when it propelled Cain to murder Abel. It was envy that drove Joseph's brothers to turn him over to the Midianites—and he spent his youth in Egyptian prisons. It was envy that induced Korah to lead a rebellion that resulted in the deaths of more than fifteen thousand Israelites. Saul was motivated by envy when he hurled the spear to kill David, who was playing the harp for him. Envy also was the motive for the crucifixion of our Lord, for we read, "It was out of envy that the chief priests had handed Jesus over" to Pilate (Mark 15:10). In Mark 7:22, Jesus linked envy with murder, adultery, and slander. God is clear and unambiguous. He says, "I will treat you in accordance with your anger and jealousy" (Ezek. 35:11). This is the behavior that was taking over the Corinthian church.

Envy, which so easily flares into murderous rage, provoked deeper and deeper strife in the Corinthian church. The Corinthians quarreled continually. They divided into factions. When the only attachment that truly mattered was their tie to Jesus Christ, some claimed to belong to Paul. Some said they belonged to Peter, and others maintained they followed Apollos. Paul pointed out that he was a fellow worker *with* Peter and Apollos. How could the people play these men off against each other? The envy and strife caused divisions, which literally means "standing apart." What is utterly astounding is that they stood apart from each other, using these leaders of the faith. They were not standing apart from sin, or sinners, or heretical sects, but from each other!

What can we do about this problem?

The Bible is clear, "Warn a divisive person once, and then warn him a second time. After that, have nothing to do with him" (Titus 3:10). Divisive people are individuals *who cause divisions in the church.* They could be pleasant and popular folks, since divisiveness has nothing to do with personality. It has to do with character. There are those people who in their antagonism for a leader of the church, or their supposed esteem for a leader, will badmouth the rest. Most people are so afraid to offend someone, even one who would divide and destroy the church, that they let such a person continue rather than confront that person and put him or her in a position to be disciplined by the church.

Two pastors who recently called me were under tremendous duress because of individuals in their separate congregations. The people creating trouble were well-liked by many. But they were disrupting the church and turning people away from the ministries that had been used to bring people to faith in Jesus Christ.

Both of these men asked me for counsel. I learned that the troublemakers had been warned repeatedly. I simply said to each of these pastors that the board of elders in their churches should put them out. Understand this: The church is *not* a place where anyone can go . . . and do anything he or she wants. Even clubs remove members who disregard the rules. The church is not a club. It is the congregation of the living and holy God. Yet we let more nonsense persist here than the most lax country club would ever consider allowing. Bring about discipline! If there is no repentance, and the person is removed as a member, instruct the congregation not to even associate with this kind of person. The reason is that such a person will use all his or her energy to violate and pollute the ministry of that church. Second Timothy 3:5 is equally strong when it speaks about such individuals, "Have nothing to do with them."

Avoid divisive behavior on your part. Don't become part of a group that exists for the purpose of complaining about everything. Avoid complaining to a willing ear—there are always people who want to hear the latest gripe. There are always people waiting to spread evil reports. I was told about a problem with someone in our church. The assumption was that I would know about this individual, because the report in question was common knowledge. Here's what's interesting— I didn't have a clue. I said, "I'm not interested. Please deal with this person yourself." When I am told things, people are surprised that I don't know about them already. They shouldn't be. When people come to me with information that I don't need to know, I don't let myself find out. Being a pastor doesn't make it right for me to be privy to things I'm not supposed to know. I recommend that practice for all people.

We are discussing the specific divisive behaviors of envy

and strife, which divide and ruin good churches. However, a quick look at the Scriptures reveals others, most notably grumbling and complaining. The most striking example in the Bible of this sin is the activity of Korah, Dathan, and Abiram. They continually grumbled and complained against the leadership of Moses. Numbers 16 said, "They rose up against Moses. With them were two hundred fifty Israelite men." These men had contempt and disrespect for God's ordained leadership, attitudes that could only kill and divide the congregation. In this case, Korah, Dathan, and Abiram had gathered others in their cause. When they came to Moses and presented their complaints, it sounded very spiritual, "You have gone too far, for the whole congregation is holy, every one of them." By saying there isn't any "them" (leaders) and "us" (congregation), they were creating chaos in the congregation. They were destroying the rule of God's people by God-appointed elders, also known as Presbyterianism. Even in the Old Covenant it was the mainstay of the congregation. They were replacing it with congregationalism, which is the rule of everyone. Because this plan was thoroughly dividing the congregation, Moses opposed it and called for God to judge. The earth swallowed up Korah, Dathan, and Abiram, and fire devoured all who followed them. This took place because of grumbling and complaining.

But this is not all—there is a related issue. Inseparable to this is fault finding, which like the previously mentioned sins can only divide the congregation as well. When individuals start finding fault and taking these faults to others, it subverts and divides the work and the ministry of the congregation. Even in the example concerning the leadership of Moses, which involved grumbling and complaining, there was fault finding. The attack against Moses was over *presumed* faults in his leadership. He was supposedly not acknowledging the holiness of everyone in the congregation. God did not view this accusation as positive criticism but as rebellion. He quashed it immediately.

Observable in this foul example as well is backbiting. When the grumblers and complainers went about their nasty business and found fault after fault, their next step was to backbite. They didn't let up on the supposed leadership weaknesses of Moses, and eventually they enlisted 250 of the leaders in the congregation to join in a rebellion to overthrow him. Remember that the purpose of this rebellion was to get rid of Moses, because he didn't elevate all of them (which of course would elevate none of them). Rebels such as Korah are not interested in elevating everyone but only in elevating themselves. Such is the way of grumblers, fault finders, complainers, and backbiters. There is no room for them in the church. They are not welcome, and their divisiveness is abominable, even if those who listen to it find it appealing.

A final divisive behavior in this discussion is heresy. Heresy is any idea that goes against the teachings of the Word of God. For example, the earliest heresy of the Old Covenant people of God came through two of its leaders, Nadab and Abihu. These men added elements to the worship of God, strange fires, that were not directly commanded by God. They taught the heretical doctrine that worship could include those things that were not commanded by God (Lev. 10:1–2). Historically, this practice has divided the church, as does every heretical teaching. God judged Nadab and Abihu for their disregard for the worship of God and consumed them by fire.

Practice the fruit of the Spirit. The ultimate remedy for divisiveness in the church is a congregation whose character is a demonstration of the fruit of the Spirit, "Love, joy, peace, patience, kindness, goodness, faithfulness, gentleness, and self-control" (Gal. 5:22–23). This passage says that those who belong to Christ live by the Spirit. This is the directive—a Spirit-lived life, which is a life with no divisiveness. The text in Galatians ends by saying that those who live by the fruit of the Spirit will not demonstrate strife or envy.

We must always watch out for the church, that its ministry is esteemed and all care is extended to guard against division. Guarding is each person's responsibility, for it is each person's responsibility not to envy others and their gifts. Remember that this envy leads to strife, which leads to grumbling, complaining, fault finding, backbiting, and even false teaching. All of these divide and destroy the church. All of these grieve the Lord, who died for his church.

Paul's hope was that everyone in the church would work toward unity, putting aside all divisive behaviors for the sake of Christ. He wanted to see the believers work positively to make changes that bless, rather than divide and destroy the church by subversive and cowardly behavior. The healthy church isn't a perfect church. It doesn't have perfect leaders or perfect members. But it works toward a oneness that glorifies Christ, and repudiates anything that would divide and tear the body asunder.

**N**ot long ago, the world was inundated with news of the disgraceful private life of the president of the United States. At the end of the deliberations in Congress, there was a remarkable public verdict voiced: "We don't care what he is in private. All we care is that he is a good president!" In fact, his approval rating soared to over 60 percent, the highest it had ever been. A senator had the audacity to suggest that these shameful practices *do* matter. He said that any CEO discovered behaving this way would have been asked to resign immediately by the board of directors. The United States Congress had a challenging decision to make regarding its response to this situation. The members were required to disapprove of his reprehensible behavior, discourage future such misconduct by those in leadership, and lead the country in the most stable way, simultaneously. They decided that he should continue to govern the nation until his term was completed (see Matt. 13:24–30).

As our society has distanced itself more and more from the

> ### 1 CORINTHIANS 5:1-5
>
> ¹It is actually reported that there is sexual immorality among you, and of a kind that does not occur even among pagans: A man has his father's wife. ²And you are proud! Shouldn't you rather have been filled with grief and have put out of your fellowship the man who did this? ³Even though I am not physically present, I am with you in spirit. And I have already passed judgment on the one who did this, just as if I were present. ⁴When you are assembled in the name of our Lord Jesus and I am with you in spirit, and the power of our Lord Jesus is present, ⁵hand this man over to Satan, so that the sinful nature may be destroyed and his spirit saved on the day of the Lord.

Word of God, it has come to approve previously unimaginable sexual practices. As much as we view this as a recent problem, it isn't! Amazingly, even this offense had become part of the Corinthian church. It was the problem that Paul addressed in these opening verses of 1 Corinthians 5. Remember that Paul had been dealing with the various transgressions that tore apart the church—the intellectual sins, the pride, the arrogance. Suddenly he encountered a sin of a whole new variety. He said, "It isn't even mentioned by the pagans." The Corinthian church wasn't in the forefront of righteousness—it was in the forefront of evil! Paul knew that evil had to be eradicated. If it went unchecked, it would destroy the church.

We know that sexual sins were common in the city of Corinth. In fact, Corinth was known for its vice. Shockingly, the church of Corinth was guilty of even *worse* sin. Paul said,

"It is actually reported that there is sexual immorality among you, and of a kind that does not occur even among the pagans." These were the people who had been shepherded by Paul, Apollos, and possibly Peter. These were individuals to whom Paul had taught the evils of such behavior. This is a church that somehow let itself engage in activity that Paul had warned could bring about its destruction (1 Cor. 3:17). The general report about this church was that it permitted such behavior. There is the sense that Paul received the report that the church allowed this destructive behavior from people outside the church! The language of 1 Corinthians 5:1 can mean, "There is nothing that is heard of among you *except* sexual immorality." There is no question that many individuals came into the church in Corinth bringing the baggage of immoral lifestyles. The problem developed when some continued this behavior as believers. Paul's teaching was clear, "Flee from sexual immorality" (1 Cor. 6:18).

People have come to the church that I pastor and left in a rage when I told them that they cannot continue in sexual immorality. They try to convince me that they are involved in relationships with godly men or women. Paul spoke clearly against the sexual immorality in Corinth. The church had a particularly heinous offense. It was that one of the members of the church was having a sexual relationship with his father's wife. (The expression "father's wife" indicates that this was not his biological mother.) This particular sin would be known as incest. In the Old Testament, it was punishable by death, as Deuteronomy 22:22 states. Leviticus 18:8 put it unmistakably, "Do not have sexual relations with your father's wife." People who persist in this lifestyle are unbelievers. The verdict upon them was clear, because Paul said in the next chapter that we must not be deceived, for they will not "inherit the kingdom of God" (1 Cor. 6:10). Why not? Because God said in 1 Thessalonians 4:3, "It is God's will that you should be sanctified." He defines this as "avoid[ing] sexual immorality." The idea is that you cannot become holy if you defile yourself in sexual sin. You are clearly going against the will of God for your life if you engage in sexual sin. Paul said much more about this in 1 Corinthians 6, but understand that if you desire to do the will of God, you need to make sure you don't commit sexual immorality.

As if this weren't bad enough, this sin was compounded by the rest of the sins of the Corinthian church. Notice how they responded to the situation. They are described in 1 Corinthians 5:2 as "proud." Instead of being distressed by this sin, they were proud. They became known throughout Corinth as the religious community that condoned any kind of vice. Paul is amazed that they thought they had any cause to boast. But this revealed another problem—their pride left them unable to see things as they really were. Instead, he said, they should have felt sorrow. They should have been broken. They should have been mourning. They should have thrown this man out of the church. That is the sense of 1 Corinthians 5:13. But they didn't. They remained proud, contemptuous, and arrogant. It was to this sin-filled, chaotic church that the apostle gave his directives.

If there is one area that is lacking in many otherwise good churches, it is the area of discipline. In many churches, discipline has never taken place. I remember a couple who came to our church in Ottawa and told me that they had been sent by their pastor to learn the Scriptures here. I called him, and he agreed about this reason for sending them to me. I decided to push him a bit, and in so doing, I discovered that they had been a real problem to him and he hoped that I would be able to deal with them. I told him that they were more than welcome here, *after* all the problems they had caused in *his* congregation were dealt with by their church. He responded with a bit of confusion, asking me, "Why would I ever send people to you who were not problems?"

I received a call from someone interested in worshiping in our church. I asked, "Why?" She answered, "Because I think my pastor and elders have made some sinful decisions." I asked her what these elders thought of her concerns. She said she didn't know because she had never broached these concerns with the leaders of the church. I urged her to work with them first.

A man from a large congregation called me for help because his wife had left him for another man. I asked what the church had done. He told me that he, his wife, and her live-in boyfriend were all worshiping in the church and nothing was being done. I told him to tell the pastor that I would be glad to speak to him. The pastor persistently refused, and since the church was independent, there was no recourse to pursue this. He would never, ever speak with me about this, even though open adultery was occurring in his church and a family was being destroyed.

My experiences of this reaction to discipline are almost endless. Many churches are just like the Corinthians. They pat themselves on the back for being a great church . . . but do nothing about sin. Jonathan Edwards was one of the most notable preachers since John Calvin. He was certainly the most influential preacher in the history of the church in the United States. This great preacher and theologian was expelled from his church by a ten-to-one vote (231 to 23). The reason, as I see it, was simple. He said that people who were involved in open, unrepentant sin could not take the Lord's Supper. He said that there was going to be discipline for sin. Let us not forget that Calvin too was hurled out of Geneva when he tried to practice discipline. He was eventually invited back, but that is the exception.

Why do churches hesitate to discipline? Well, if Jonathan Edwards and John Calvin can be thrown out of their churches, how many pastors are safe? They hope that they can keep peace by not confronting sin. The denomination in which I am a pastor has a similar story. The minister who brought me into this denomination had just begun his work in Syracuse, New York. There were only a few people in the congregation, as it was an old and dying church. One of these few people happened to be the exceedingly wealthy president of one of New York's largest banks. He came to the pastor to remind him that his job in Syracuse depended upon his doing things the way he demanded, to which this pastor replied, "Perish with your silver and your gold." The man left. The pastor never saw this man again until he was asked by the family to officiate at the man's funeral, by which time the Syracuse church was filled to capacity. I remember one of my students from our seminary in Ottawa embarking on his first ministry in another old, dying church. He was told almost the first week to "remember who's paying your check." He spoke to me about this, and this individual was rebuked for such sinful behavior. Elders too should be known as those who support the discipline of the church, because of their love and concern for those who need to be corrected.

The church should not hesitate to discipline. It should never tolerate immorality. Situations of unrepentant sin and immorality should be disciplined. We read in Ephesians 5 that there is not even to be a hint of sexual immorality and that we are to have nothing to do with the fruitless deeds of darkness but rather to rebuke them. Matthew 18:15 instructs that you do this first person to person. If the individual doesn't listen, take another person with you. Finally, you bring it to the elders of the church. There is another principle here that is important. If the sin is private, affecting one or two people, that is as far as it should be exposed in dealing with it. If it is a public offense, only then do you publicly discipline an individual. The principle is that you should go only as far as you must go to bring about a resolution to the matter. Specifically, here is what we see in 1 Corinthians 5:3–5.

1. There is not to be a fear of judging sin. This is not the same judgment we read about in Matthew 7:1, where we are told, "Do not judge, or you too will be judged." Church discipline is the rightful judging of sin. Don't be frightened when people want to prevent judgment because they are friends with someone or are a family member. If there is unrepentant, unrelenting sin, it must be judged. In Corinth, this man continued to have an incestuous relationship, and the apostle said he had already passed judgment on him. The judgment of sin is to be handled without fear of man.

2. The church is assembled. When the church must expel, or excommunicate, someone, the church members, by their presence, endorse the edict. The elders speak for the church as a whole. The church supports the excommunication by obeying its elders and not associating with the unrepentant person.

3. It is in the name of our Lord Jesus. Any judicial pro-
   ceeding must occur under the sponsorship, director-
   ship, oversight, and with the character of Christ. If it
   is to promote Christ and his name, it must be with his
   character—it is to be done as he would do it.

4. It is done in the power of the Lord Jesus—with the authority of Jesus Christ. When people mock the courts
   of Christ, they are mocking Christ. This is what the
   idea of "two or three gathered in his name" is all about.
   This expression is not a directive for a prayer meeting.
   It is instructive for church discipline. It follows the
   most important passage in the Bible that speaks about
   discipline, Matthew 18. It amplifies it by speaking of
   Christ's power to the church, "Whatever you bind on
   earth will be bound in heaven, and whatever you loose
   on earth will be loosed in heaven. Again, I tell you,
   that if two of you on earth agree about anything you
   ask for, it will be done for you by my Father in heaven.
   For where two or three come together in my name,
   there am I with them" (Matt. 18:18–19). Again, the
   two agreeing on earth about anything are the elders
   agreeing on the above-mentioned discipline, and thus
   it is done. That is *the power of the Lord Jesus.* That is
   what the church has—nothing less than the power of
   Jesus Christ at its disposal. It is a power it almost never
   uses, even when it is called for.

5. "Hand this man over to Satan." This is a metaphor for
   "excommunicate him." Excommunication is so serious that it is the abandonment of the person to Satan.
   While the individual is given over to the evil that he
   clings to, it is the hope of the church that this situa-

tion will not be his final estate but that he will be restored.

6. ". . . so that the sinful nature may be destroyed and his spirit saved on the day of the Lord." It is a purpose expressed here that being under the power of the devil might awaken this man to the truth and power of Christ. It is the hope that his commitment to sin might be eradicated and that like a newborn believer he will be committed to Christ, and in that commitment be saved.

7. "The day of the Lord." There is a terminus to this responsibility to discipline. That end is the day of the Lord. The church must exercise discipline only until the end, and then it is over for all eternity. So the church, and its leaders in particular, should be encouraged to carry out their responsibility knowing that it will come to an end when the Lord comes for his people.

All of this is tremendously important for God's people for several reasons.

1. *Restoration.* The goal of godly discipline is to restore the offender.

2. *Justice.* Church discipline is the only way to provide justice in the church. With church discipline, it is not anything goes, but rather, those who refuse to heed the Word of God will be disciplined.

3. *Protection.* The innocent are protected in the church when discipline is practiced. Protection is a reality that should belong to all of God's people in the church.

This is not always the case, and the weaker members of the church are often left vulnerable. When the leaders of the church exercise discipline, the sheep know they are protected, the fences are up, and the wolves are kept out.

4. *Safety.* Church discipline is the only way to ensure safety. You are safe in the church. While elders may seem to let certain situations go for a while, in a good church they are keeping watch. They know that they must never allow anyone to harm the church, so they are prepared to stop harmful behavior in a moment. Let me put it this way. Everyone has some degree of personal problems. The leaders must not let them become a snare for the church. The sheep are to graze in safety. The elders must be committed to making the church an environment of peace and joy.

5. *Fear of the Lord.* Knowing about such matters as these, it is altogether wise for you to fear the Lord, because you know sin will not be tolerated. During a recent discipline situation in our church, one of our elders reminisced with me about his earliest days in the church. Many years earlier, when he and his wife had just come to the church, I had made a pastoral visit during a time when serious discipline was being carried out. He remembered my saying to him, "If you join this church and involve yourself in sin, you will be disciplined." We recalled his response, "That's why I want to be here." A biblical approach to discipline is an encouragement to all who fear the Lord.

6. *Edification.* Indeed, the spiritual edification of the congregation takes place when their hearts are com-

mitted to obedience to Christ. They grow in grace, because they are no longer rebels who only do what's right in their own eyes but instead are those who do all to please God. They know that if the elders demand their allegiance to the Lord, so too the Lord expects a complete commitment.

7. *Representation.* The church is God's kingdom on earth—the place where his righteousness dwells. It represents him! It must represent him accurately to the world.

Our society has been distancing its morality from the Word of God in recent times, but that is not a new occurrence in history. Even the Corinthian church, centuries ago, had problems of immorality. Since God is the head of the church and requires purity in his house, immoral behavior must be disciplined. Redeemed sinners, to remain in the church, must live holy lives. This does not mean that they do not sin, but it means that when they do sin, they confess their sins to God and strive even more for that holiness, for "without holiness no one will see the Lord" (Heb. 12:14). When believers stumble deeply, the church is to imitate the Lord, who "disciplines those he loves" (Heb. 12:6). We know, as Hebrews teaches us, that while "no discipline seems pleasant at the time. . . . Later on, however, it produces a harvest of righteousness and peace for those who have been trained by it" (Heb. 12:11). Rejoice that you seek to walk righteously. Rejoice that you are sons and daughters who are disciplined when you stumble and fall. Rejoice that when your church faces unrepentant sin, it will do what it must do to preserve the righteousness of Christ and restore the soul of the one in sin.

C ivil action against the church of Jesus Christ is fairly uncommon in our day. I have been an ordained minister of the gospel since November 10, 1978, so I have been in the ministry for twenty-five years. During this time I have seen a diversity of situations and have pastored people whose problems encompassed every genre of sins and grief experienced by humanity. I have been asked by secular courts to counsel parents who murdered their child. I have ministered to women who have been assaulted. I have worked with homosexuals, repentant and unrepentant. I have counseled women who have had abortions. My ministry has been to countless families who have experienced the gamut of problems. I even advised a teenager whose name was Attila and whose mother introduced him by saying, "This is Attila. Hun, tell him everything." So, I've even counseled Attila the Hun!

I've had a number of serious and difficult disciplinary cases over the years in my congregation. But of all the things in which I have participated, only one involved a discipline sit-

### 1 CORINTHIANS 6:1-8

¹If any of you has a dispute with another, dare he take it before the ungodly for judgment instead of before the saints? ²Do you not know that the saints will judge the world? And if you are to judge the world, are you not competent to judge trivial cases? ³Do you not know that we will judge angels? How much more the things of this life! ⁴Therefore, if you have disputes about such matters, appoint as judges even men of little account in the

uation in which the secular legal establishment had been enlisted to fight against the church. What made this so poignant was a reflection on how vigorously the Word of God condemns such action on the part of those who are members of the church. It seems to be occurring with increasing frequency in the church, just as it happened in Corinth. It is essential to know what to do when those who are the subjects of church discipline go against Scripture to the secular legal establishment.

In the case where I was asked to help, the secular lawyer who fought against the church stated that if the church didn't do things exactly as he demanded, we "who are nothing but an administrative tribunal in the eyes of the law" would have action instituted against us forthwith and without further notice! Because the church was seeking to address members of the church of Christ biblically, these individuals had determined to take the church to a civil court and in some way bring charges against *us*. Paul addressed this exact situation in these verses by dispelling any doubt that such action on the part of people in the church is unbiblical and sinful.

church! ⁵I say this to shame you. Is it possible that there is nobody among you wise enough to judge a dispute between believers? ⁶But instead, one brother goes to law against another—and this in front of unbelievers!

⁷The very fact that you have lawsuits among you means you have been completely defeated already. Why not rather be wronged? Why not rather be cheated? ⁸Instead, you yourselves cheat and do wrong, and you do this to your brothers.

It is interesting to note that in this passage, 1 Corinthians 6, there is the most comprehensive statement in the Scriptures on the issue of taking a brother or sister to a secular court. The verdict in the Bible is clear—there is no ambiguity. Paul said, "If any one of you has a dispute with another, dare he take it before the ungodly for judgment instead of before the saints?" (1 Cor 6:1). In the case that was before one of our churches, I trembled from fear of God that people could permit such statements from the pen of their lawyer. He did not represent himself but *them*. I had never seen such contempt. These people were determined to fight the church—and the weapons they decided to use were the weapons of the world! God forbids this practice, and when it is employed, those using it are in contempt of court—God's court. They are despising of the power, rule, and authority of Almighty God.

This is precisely what Paul faced. This was another sin that was commonplace in Corinth. Just previously, Paul had declared the power of the church to "judge those inside." To their deepening shame, the Corinthians *did not* judge those inside but instead brought judgments to heathen courts. This was the church that Paul said would one day judge the world but couldn't judge itself!

Paul then said, "Appoint as judges even men of little account in the church." This can mean one of four things. Either he spoke sarcastically about lawyers, saying that the least esteemed in the church are better equipped than the best heathen lawyers to judge the matters of the church. Or he seriously meant that even the least in the church are more qualified than a pagan court. He could have been saying, "Appoint men who have no esteem in the eyes of the *world's* tribunals." Finally, it could be understood as a question, "Do you appoint those who are least esteemed by the church, in other words, the heathen?" Within the context of this letter, the reading that seems most probable is the fourth. In this light, Paul was asking, "Can you possibly make these important judgments about spiritual matters using heathen lawyers and judges?" These are people whom the church views with contempt, in terms of their ability to spiritually discern.

The answer from the Corinthians was a resounding yes! This demonstrated just how given over to sin they were. The Corinthians' behavior should have left them, as Paul said, ashamed of themselves, knowing that there must have been wise men among them who were able to judge.

You might ask why people go to lawyers when they are faced with discipline. I believe they go when they are guilty and want to confuse the issue. All they have to do is hire a lawyer, who is paid to provide a paper trail covering every technicality imaginable. When we hire pagan counsel, we become a spectacle to the world. The apostle Paul said, "You yourselves cheat and do wrong, and you do this to your brothers." Paul said you should prefer to be wronged and accept it rather than go to the heathen for their legal counsel.

In our situation, after one brief note to us, the lawyer demanded that he get what he had requested. He threatened that if he didn't, he would take us to civil court. Most people would be frightened and capitulate. But the church of Christ is not based on fear and threats. Rather, it is based on truth and love. Such threats to the people of God should strengthen their resolve against evil. In our denomination the rules are clear: "No person shall be permitted to act as counsel who is not a member of the church and subject to the jurisdiction of its courts" (*Book of Discipline*, Reformed Presbyterian Church, chapter 4, paragraph 3). In the disputes that every church has, there is no excuse to go to the heathen for their legal expertise and adjudication. In the case that was before our church court, there was the intention of taking the entire session to a heathen court. It would be wrongdoing against the entire court of the church.

From what we have said so far, one could assume that there is never a legal matter for which a church member should go to the civil magistrate. There are judgments that pertain to issues over which the church has been granted authority, and we must settle these ourselves. But the church doesn't have unlimited authority. For example, we must judge in cases such as contempt of the officers, stealing, adultery, and so on. In a marriage where there has been adultery and no repentance and reconciliation, God makes allowance for divorce because of the hardness of human hearts. The state also has something to say, or as their language puts it, they have a compelling interest. We are under the law of the land. We cannot and should not avoid that. If there are children in a divorce, especially if one spouse is living a wicked life, the believing spouse should definitely do all he or she can to secure custody of the children. If a husband beats his wife, I counsel her to go to the state and seek criminal charges against him. We in the church would deal with him biblically at the same time. If criminal charges need to be brought for criminal actions that cannot be dealt with by the church, then the state is to receive our appeal, for we must always remember that we are not given the power of the sword. At the same time, where we must legislate and adjudicate, we must never allow the state to take that power.

This gives Christians valuable tools to help them face evil. If you respect those who rule in the church, you will not step out from the duly constituted process of church discipline. This kind of thinking helps you to realize the power of the saints. In 1 Corinthians 6:2 it says that the saints will judge the world, and 1 Corinthians 6:3 says that we will judge angels. This being the case, there should be a realization and confidence that the rulers of the church are capable of judging what Paul calls "trivial cases." These are the cases we face in the church, all of which are trivial in comparison with judging angels. If we are to judge angels, Paul said, "how much more the things of this life!" But applying this depends on whether God's people break the pattern of this age, which is to be enamored with the secular, while despising what God has made holy. To be true to the calling of respecting church courts, several things are necessary.

1. *Recognize the authority of the rulers in the church.* The church must appoint as rulers men who have fulfilled all the requirements of the Scriptures. These men,

when carefully chosen from the body of Christ, possess the authority of Christ, an authority that must be recognized and respected. These are the men given the authority of Matthew 18:18 to bind and loose. Recognizing this, the church must not despise them. The most basic way to uphold them in their office is not to go to heathen lawyers, for the heathen cannot possibly respect or recognize the power and authority of the church court, an authority to bind on earth and know that it is bound in heaven. This, my friends, is the church. It is the court in which Jesus Christ sovereignly rules over his citizens. It is the court in which he expects his people, not the heathen, to judge.

2. *Remember the glory of God.* Paul made it clear that when brothers and sisters in Christ go to the civil magistrate to be their lawyers and judges, they bring shame and disrepute on the body of Christ. You do this, he said, "in front of unbelievers," and the unbelievers see that the church is unable to function. This behavior in Corinth showed their contempt of the church. Instead, the heathen authorities should learn something from believers when they see that there is authority in the church.

3. *Rather be wronged.* Why not rather be cheated than take a brother or sister to a court of law? This point is a very real matter of faith, because here is where you are tested to see if you really believe that God will take care of you. When you've been wronged, the natural impulse is to demand your full due, and if you don't get it, to go to a heathen court to demand it rather than accept a wrong against you. But God does grant

justice to his people. Poet Henry Wadsworth Longfellow wrote,

Though the mill of God grinds slowly,
Yet it grinds exceeding small.
Though with patience He stands waiting,
With exactness grinds He all.

For scriptural examples of God's justice, remember the story of Joseph in Genesis. Not only did God raise him up as a vizier of Egypt after his brothers had brought him low as a slave, but also God used Joseph to save his people. Because of that, the Israelites were preserved, and generations later Christ, our Savior, was born. Behold, the justice and mercy of God! The story of Esther also demonstrates God's incredible justice and mercy to his people. Though the name of God is never mentioned in the Book of Esther, the hand of God clearly moves to preserve the lives of those who love him and also to bring justice to those who defy him.

What is so wrong with going outside the church for judgment? First, it indicates a deep disrespect for the leaders. It says, "The secular experts can do it better." It looks to worldly competence rather than the judgment of the leaders who have the Spirit of God! Second, it indicates a lack of belief in God. It is God who rules his church. It is God who put the leaders in place and who guides them. Third, it despises the *role* of the leaders. They are the undershepherds who represent God. Is it serious for a nation to despise an ambassador? For a citizen to scorn a policeman? Why? Because they represent the powers behind them. How much more serious it is to disrespect church leaders and despise the God who placed them there!

When Ananias and Sapphira lied to the church leaders in Acts 5, they were really lying to God, as the apostle Peter said. God immediately struck them dead. Church leaders are not in place to advance their pet interests. They have an entrustment. They will answer to God for how they lead. May God give all of his people faith to obey their leaders and courage to exercise godly discipline when it is necessary.

**R**ecently my wife and I met with a woman who, knowing that I was trained as a psychologist, wanted to tell me a recurring dream she had been having. After she recounted it to us, I responded, "It sounds like you are dealing with someone who is in big trouble." This lady teaches thirteen-year-old boys and girls in a public school. She said, "Yes, there's this boy in my class. I'm really concerned for him and a thirteen-year-old girl, with whom he is involved sexually." As we talked further, I discovered that there were additional similar situations that worried her, and she began to realize that these were causing the nightmares she was having every night. This woman, while not a Christian, knew that these behaviors were wrong. Yet she wasn't sure how to deal with them, so she had nightmares about these kids, who were seriously damaging their lives at twelve and thirteen years of age. These are kids who have been taught that this behavior is sanctioned, condoned, and approved, even though most

**1 CORINTHIANS 6:12–20**

¹²"Everything is permissible for me"—but not everything is beneficial. "Everything is permissible for me"—but I will not be mastered by anything. ¹³"Food for the stomach and the stomach for food"—but God will destroy them both. The body is not meant for sexual immorality, but for the Lord, and the Lord for the body. ¹⁴By his power God raised the Lord from the dead, and he will raise us also. ¹⁵Do you not know that your bodies are members of Christ himself? Shall I then take the members of Christ and unite them with a prostitute?

thinking people believe it destroys not only life but community as well.

A young man I'll call Steve came to me for counseling. He was a professing Christian and had been encouraged to get help. He told me that he is a homosexual, and that while others had encouraged him to repent and change, he didn't see the need. He then cited a biblical text as support for his determination to continue his homosexual behavior, "As the Bible teaches, 'All things are lawful.'" Certainly in Corinth they held that view. Is it true? Did Paul mean to say that because we are Christians we can do *whatever* we want? This issue erupted in controversy at several points in the Corinthian church. Many in the church uncritically accepted the sexual immorality there, so that at one point a man who was involved sexually with his father's wife was allowed to go on without discipline until the apostle Paul intervened. What is involved here? How are we to understand it?

Never! [16]Do you not know that he who unites himself with a prostitute is one with her in body? For it is said, "The two will become one flesh." [17]But he who unites himself with the Lord is one with him in spirit.

[18]Flee from sexual immorality. All other sins a man commits are outside his body, but he who sins sexually sins against his own body. [19]Do you not know that your body is a temple of the Holy Spirit, who is in you, whom you have received from God? You are not your own; [20]you were bought at a price. Therefore honor God with your body.

## LAWFUL AND BENEFICIAL

There is an injunction in 1 Corinthians 6:9 that speaks clearly to the issue we are examining. It says, "Do not be deceived. Neither the sexually immoral nor idolaters nor adulterers nor male prostitutes nor homosexual offenders [practicing this lifestyle] nor thieves nor drunkards nor slanderers nor swindlers will inherit the kingdom of God." Seen from this context, did Paul mean to suggest that you can do *anything* you want? If he did, then the homosexual can continue in homosexuality, the adulterer in adultery, the fornicator in fornication, and the murderer can even continue in murder! We know at the outset that Paul would never suggest that as a Christian any behavior is acceptable. Then what did he mean?

I believe it is simple. All things were permissible for him *that had been declared lawful in the Scriptures.* Paul presented his argument this way because he would not even do all those things that were lawful for him to do. Instead, he made a careful determination. He concluded that while all things that are biblically lawful are indeed permissible, some things that are lawful are not beneficial. He used a word that means that not all things he is allowed to do would contribute to what is good. If he determined that this was the case in a specific instance, he would refrain from doing even the things he was *allowed* by God to do.

Perhaps you may be wondering, "What could possibly be an example of such a situation as that?" Paul gave us a perfect example in 1 Corinthians 8 of something that was allowable but that he wouldn't do. There he spoke about eating meats offered to idols. His point was simple. "I can eat any meat that is offered to an idol, because an idol is nothing. There is only one living and true God. But I will never eat meat again if my brother happens to be a very young believer out of strict Jewish orthodoxy and would be aghast and sickened at the thought of eating meat that was offered to an idol" (author's paraphrase). Another translation of the key words in this text gives a slightly different idea, but with the same thrust: "All things are in my power, but I will not be overpowered by anything."

With this as a background, we can understand what Paul was thinking when he went on to speak about sexual sin. He was dealing with one of the most enslaving sins. It is a sin that knows no limits for rationalization. If you don't believe that sexual sin can enslave, then you are not aware of what is going on around you! I'm convinced that sexual sin enslaves, and this is my experience from counseling thousands of people. In fact, sexual sin enslaves with a power that may be greater than heroin. People's lives are destroyed because of enslavement to sex. Marriages and families are destroyed because of enslavement to sex. There is little worse than seeing people destroyed by their passions. It is, sadly, even in the Christian church. How we determine to deal with this matter will deeply affect the whole Christian church.

Paul was not *abrogating*, that is *doing away with*, the moral code that had been the hallmark of believers throughout the ages and saying instead that you can do whatever you want. In fact, I suggest to you that he was tightening it. He was saying that a true believer *does not even exercise all the freedom he has.*

This brought Paul to the heart of his concern. He spoke first of foods and the stomach. His point was simple. Foods in the stomach are going to pass away, but the body *in its entirety* will not. The Corinthians had been teaching that they could, because of the grace of Christ, do as they pleased. Notice again that one example of this was in the area of food. They believed that eating had nothing to do with their character or spiritual life—that they were free with regard to foods. They were wrong even there, because this is not an example of *adiaphora*, a thing *indifferent*. They were not free to be gluttons. They were not free to eat things that would destroy their bodies. Though they weren't free even in regard to food, they extended their argument to say that just as food did not hinder spirituality (which was a wrong conclusion), neither did sexual promiscuity hinder spirituality. "We are free!" was their cry. Just as the body is not meant for gluttony, Paul also forcefully states in this passage that the body is not meant for sexual immorality.

The city of Corinth was much like our contemporary culture. It was consumed and obsessed with sex. Everywhere you turned, sex was there. Corinth was such a sexual capital that the common expression at the time, "to Corinthianize," meant "to go to a prostitute." The church had to face the pressure of how to deal with the sexual latitude and promiscuity that pervaded a culture and soon after infected the church. Little by little, the Corinthian Christians heard how stupid it was to condemn extramarital sex. They heard that they were being old-fashioned, that they were being fastidious, that they were being unaccepting of other people, that they were adding something to being a Christian that wasn't intended, that they were destroying their freedom. They were worn down.

Just as church after church and denomination after denomination has been worn down on issue after issue today, so too the Corinthians were being worn down. They came to accept the culture rather than working counter to it and speaking against the prevailing mindset of the culture. They came to embody the culture and embrace the culture. They ceased being a countercultural people. They ceased being a people who upheld God's verdict that he created the body, as he says in this text, "not for fornication." They became unwilling to submit to the biblical teaching that the body is not for any kind of sexual immorality, as was witnessed by their acceptance of the man who had an immoral relationship with his stepmother.

## BODY AND SPIRIT

An early heresy to plague the Christian church was known as Gnosticism. One of its teachings was that Christianity is a *spiritual* religion—it has nothing to do with anything *physical*. Since it is focused on the spirit, it doesn't matter what you do with your body. But what the Gnostics, and so many others who aren't even familiar with Gnosticism, are guilty of is a failure to appreciate the significance of the body. It is this body that God will raise on the last day. It is this body, God said in this text, that is a member of Christ. It is because of the *exalted* place of the body that we are told to "Flee from sexual immorality. All other sins a man commits are outside his body, but he who sins sexually sins against his own body" (1 Corinthians 6:18).

Why is this important? The next two verses answer that question. "Do you not know that your body is a temple of the Holy Spirit, who is in you, whom you have received from God? You are not your own; you were bought at a price. Therefore honor God with your body." People are harmed physically and spiritually when they sin sexually because of who and what they are. Unbelievers are harmed because they have turned themselves into creatures who live by instinct and not conscience, and certainly not the standard of the Word of God. They have cheapened themselves, and that is invariably painful when they realize that they have sold their purity for something worthless. That purity is more valuable than any passing pleasure. It hurts believers even more than unbelievers because they know who they are. They know they are temples of the living God, yet they choose to ignore God. They choose to go their own way. How can that do anything but hurt?

I would venture to say that sexual immorality has destroyed more families than drugs and alcohol combined, and I will tell you why. Drugs and alcohol tear a person apart, and that of course will eventually affect the rest of the family. But adultery is the direct tearing apart, in its very action, of the marriage bond, even when your spouse doesn't know what damage is done. It doesn't depend upon an agreement or an understanding or both knowing for damage to occur. There's damage because we can't help being who we are, and we can't help destroying each other when we sin in this way. This is why Proverbs speaks of adultery as suicidal (Prov. 7:23).

Can God heal and restore marriages that have been thus harmed? Absolutely! By his incredible grace a couple can accept and imitate the forgiveness of Christ and depend on him for strength from moment to moment to move on. It is a crushing event like others in life that teaches a child of God that his strength is from him alone, and not from a marriage or a comfortable life, or a good self-image. Adultery is a grief that does experience healing with time, as other griefs do. It is a path that some of God's children will travel but not a route that any, looking back, would choose for themselves.

The Corinthians, in their misunderstanding about sex, failed to see the great freedom they had as Christians. Freedom for Paul was serving Christ! After being enslaved to the kingdom opposing Christ, it was with joy that he was forgiven and made free to serve the living God. Freedom was never meant to be doing everything he could do. It was *relinquishment.* Freedom for Paul meant relinquishing whatever stood in the way of the advance of the gospel. Christian freedom is something you hear about in numerous Christian circles. But Paul is preaching that the greatest freedom is self-control. We are free when we flee from what might even be a hint of immorality. We are free when we treat our body as the temple of the Holy Spirit, and not a vessel for self-satisfaction. Paul said plainly in 1 Corinthians 9:27 that he "beat [his] body" and made it his slave. He said he did this "so that after I have preached to others, I myself will not be disqualified for the prize" (1 Cor. 9:27). He knew the dangers. He knew the snares.

The church is littered with preachers who were disqualified because they did not control their bodies. In the church, one very rarely hears about a preacher being disqualified because he is a drug addict or an alcoholic, although it is not unknown. But every day, preachers and their ministries are destroyed because of sexual sin. Paul said in 1 Thessalonians 4:3, "It is God's will that you should be sanctified." That is real freedom, to be sanctified, to be conformed to Christ. Then he elaborated on what he meant, "That you should avoid sexual immorality, that each of you should learn to control his own body in a way that is holy and honorable, not in passionate lust like the heathen."

This is what freedom means. It is the exercise of self-control in every area that could ever enslave you, especially in the area of sex. Your body is to be under your control. You were not created and redeemed to be *under* the control of your body. It is a style of freedom against which the Corinthian church bridled. This was sad, because the instruction of Paul could have radically changed their lives. If they had listened, Paul would never have had to warn them in his subsequent letter that a disciplinary visit was imminent.

## Complete Purity

The biblical view of sex is not prudish. Though society says that morality is a private and personal decision, the Bible is definitive. It elevates sex as something so great and special that it can be enjoyed only by a husband and his wife. Sex is not, as our culture indicates, just some biological activity that has no ramifications. This is a total lie! Just ask the women who have been used sexually and allowed themselves to be used. Ask them if it's just some physical thing to them now as they look back on it, or if it isn't, instead, something that has torn them up and broken their hearts? Just ask the men and women who have caught their spouses in adultery. See if they said, "Don't even apologize. It's just a biological act." This is nonsense. Underneath the ideology of our culture, there is a staunch adherence to standards, which, when they are broken, tear the fabric of our families and our nations apart. This idea that sex is a physical act like eating or sleeping is a lie foisted on a culture so that people could have free access to sex and have no inhibitions about it and absolutely no guilt. This was the idea of the sexual revolution, and it has destroyed the lives of a generation of people.

Young people often believe that they can fool around sexually and not be hurt. If you think this way, you are only fooling yourself. Christian young people often ask me how far they can go, not even realizing that once you are on that road, it can lead only to harm. This is not because sex is bad but because it is so powerful and can easily destroy what is so good. When you try to possess this enjoyment in a relationship outside of marriage, it will bring destruction.

The Scriptures are clear. They teach that young men are to treat young women "as sisters, with absolute purity" (1 Tim. 5:2). The reality is, you are to behave with a young woman the way that you would behave with your sister. You are to act with total purity. That is the standard for young men and young women: complete purity. If you start to fool around sexually even a little bit, there is only one place it will lead— into trouble and disgrace. Like a narcotic addict, you will demand more and more. You will whine and complain. You will manipulate until you get it. You will justify and rationalize everything in response to all that you have ever learned or believed, when you have convinced your boyfriend or girlfriend to give in (although it is almost always the boy convincing the girl, who foolishly believes he loves her). When she gives herself to him, then he loses interest in her or is disgusted with her and has nothing more to do with her. If there is love in the relationship, you will respect each other enough to wait for marriage. If you find yourself even thinking in the direction of sex, you had better ask yourself why you are not thinking about marriage. If you are thinking about marriage, it should be with serious-mindedness and the intention of establishing a Christian home.

Some of my readers have already been involved in sexual sin. It is important to remember that God will forgive your sin. He says about himself that he is "faithful and just and will forgive our sins and purify us from all unrighteousness" (1 John 1:9). You can be forgiven, even now, if you confess these sins. God will forgive you. But before you ever enter into such sin, please understand that you can't just say, "Well, I can do this because I will be forgiven. All I have to do is confess and repent of it." There is a very high price to pay. Nobody escapes without a price in this area. There's no free sex. That's the biggest lie of all. Be warned.

At this point you may be dealing with lust. If you give in to sin, you will deal with terrible guilt. Sometimes this guilt can destroy your life. There is guilt connected with giving yourself to some guy who's a creep, who gets what he wants, leaving you afterward experiencing only betrayal and shame. There is the guilt connected with having dreams and hopes for the future, yet having no way to finish your education. I spoke recently to a talented young lady in our congregation. I warned her to stay away from a man who brought her to his room when no one was around. I told her she was going to wind up pregnant and would never do what she had dreamed and planned on doing. She refused to speak to me again, telling people that I was harsh and judgmental about this wonderful young man. Then one day I was told that she was pregnant. The very things I warned her about happened. There is also the guilt connected with having a child and feeling obligated to put that child up for adoption. Even when you believe that it would be a better home than you would be able to provide for this child, still the guilt connected with never knowing that child, or the grief of not having the delight of that child in your home and in your life, is substantial. In the heat of sexual passion these things are far from you, but they are never far from happening. Speak to people who have been deceived by sexual sin and destroyed by it. See for yourself if they don't corroborate what I am saying.

By contrast, there are couples who marry and rear the child that God has chosen to create. Though there are losses and adjustments, there is still the blessing of God on a marriage and family who are seeking to do his will. There is a sense of priority for the couple that is facing responsibly what has now become their task in life. Their child will have security in knowing his birth parents and knowing that they cared enough about him to put his life first, ahead of other goals and desires they had in life. There are also devoted mothers who rear their child alone, and grandparents and other generous people who care enough for a child to love him and take him as their responsibility, no matter what the struggles are. God will be their Helper and Provider, and they will experience the challenges and blessings of sharing life with that child. Other disappointments will be small in comparison with the privilege of being able to love and live with this small person created in the image of God.

Young men, if you are unmarried and participate in creating a child, the decisions for the life of that child will not be in your hands. You will not be given the power to decide if your child is given death or life, and if life, what that life would be. Don't put yourself in such a grievous situation! Don't treat the young women in your life in such a way as to live with regrets. Be strong men of faith whose lives are always aware of the presence of God.

If you are involved in sexual sin and you don't know Christ, the first thing I urge you to do is repent of your unbelief and trust Jesus Christ. He will make you a new person and that means chaste again. I know that's hard to comprehend. Sometimes when I've counseled women who have been harmed this way they say they feel that they can never be clean again. They feel filthy and stained. Here is what is so amazing. When you come to Jesus Christ, he makes you clean. He promises that. No matter how bad your sin, he says you will be his "holy and blameless" bride (Eph. 5:26–27). That's the promise in Christ. I urge you to take hold of him, to trust him, to be cleansed, to be made pure, and to let him enable you from this point on to live a life of purity.

## Be on Guard

There is also a warning to us all. There is no one above falling in this area. Paul warned the church, "So, if you think you are standing firm, be careful that you don't fall!" (1 Cor. 10:12). Everyone should be vigilant regarding this sin. Everyone should be on guard and should do all that's necessary to stay pure. For example, in Proverbs the young man made his first mistake not when he went to the prostitute but when he passed the place where the prostitutes lived.

I remember when we were in Amsterdam and I was ministering with a mission organization in that city. I argued with them because I disagreed with the location of their ministry— in the heart of the red-light district. Our young family found itself in the middle of Sodom. We walked through the streets covering our eyes and covering the eyes of our children. We refused to look at the pawns of this miserable sex trade that flourished in this old and beautiful city. For the few days that we had to be there, I pleaded with our hosts to consider what they were doing in that spot. I reasoned with them that there were husbands and wives and children living there in that ministry. The prostitutes, I reminded them, didn't even live there. They came for the day, or for the night, and then went back to the suburbs. Yet these missionaries were allowing their families to be polluted by this environment. Finally a young girl spoke up and said that she had been raped the other night while walking down the street trying to minister and evangelize. Though she was unwise to be alone, apparently in this environment there was no margin for error, and she too became a victim of the evils promoted there.

In Proverbs, while it is a different scenario, there is the same concern about being in the wrong places. Here, the young man made his first mistake when he passed her corner, for she was ready for him. Proverbs says, "Do not go near the door of her house, lest you give your best strength to others" (Prov. 5:8–9). You see, the idea isn't only that at the moment of complete temptation you should have the ability to say no, but rather that you should not put yourself anywhere near the path of such temptation in the first place! You should not go to a young man's or a young woman's house alone. I won't even counsel any young woman without someone else being present. Why? Because I know that the heart is deceitful and desperately sick (Jer. 17:9), and I don't exclude my heart from that.

The danger of adultery is aptly described in Proverbs 6:26, where it says that a man's life will be "reduce[d] to a loaf of bread." Proverbs 5 also speaks. The adulterer says of himself, groaning at the end of his life, with flesh and body spent, "I hated discipline! How my heart spurned correction! I would not obey my teachers or listen to my instructors. I have come tho the brink of utter ruin in the midst of the whole assembly" (Prov. 5:12–14). He was saying that not only did adultery ruin him physically, but also it brought disgrace on him in the congregation. You know, many times I hear Christians say, "Why does the church get so upset about sexual sins? Sin is sin, and this sin is no worse than any other sin." But this is not true. Some sins are worse than other sins. Some sins are crimes, while some are not. Some of those sins and crimes demand your life. Some demand a twofold restitution, some demand fourfold restitution, and others even demand sevenfold restitution. Would you dare suggest that there's no gradation, that some sins are not worse than others, and therefore do not have worse consequences?

Lust is a sin. It is an immoral thought in your heart. Is this as serious as then going out and committing adultery? James said, "Desire . . . gives birth to sin, and sin . . . gives birth to death" (James 1:15). He was not teaching here that lust is not sin. He was simply teaching that sin can eventually can become irreversible. Can you really believe that lust is just as bad as committing adultery? Is it true, "I've done it already in my heart, I might as well go and do it in my life"? May God banish such sinful illogic from our minds! In Proverbs 6 it speaks of the husband whose wife has committed adultery with another man: "He will show no mercy when he takes revenge. He will not accept any compensation [not even sevenfold]; he will refuse the bribe, however great it is" (Prov. 6:34–35). The strongest argument against adultery is given in Proverbs 5. Here the question is simply, why would you consider committing adultery, "when a man's ways are in full view of the LORD, and he examines all his paths" (Prov. 5:21)? You can't hide your sin from the Lord, even if no one else sees.

This sin is so bad that it is a desecration of the temple. Society does acknowledge that destroying a place of worship is a terrible thing. It is unacceptable to desecrate a house of worship. That is what we do when we desecrate our bodies, which are temples of the Holy Spirit. It is a despising of our redemption. It is, as Proverbs 6:32 says, a demonstration of a complete lack of judgment and an action of self-destruction.

Is marriage the answer to sexual temptation? It is true that the Scriptures teach that marriage is the appropriate and only acceptable relationship for sexual interaction. In a relationship that cares and loves and has mutual affection, the sexual relationship will be a delight. Even problems are an occasion to express commitment and work together. That, however, does not mean there will be no sexual temptations. The Scripture connects the sin of adultery with the sin of greed. In other words, though a person has everything he or she could need, that person covets more. The story of King David's adultery is a perfect example. The motivation for his adultery was brought home by the story told by Nathan the prophet (2 Sam. 12:1–13). Though King David was abundantly blessed by the generous hand of the Lord beyond what he needed, he still took what belonged to someone else. This makes the verse more poignant than ever, which says that the man who commits adultery is reduced to a loaf of bread (Prov. 6:26). When the Lord provides, he provides generously, but if we are not happy with that and go against his commandments to get more for ourselves, we will be reduced to nothing but bare survival. If the Lord blesses us with a husband or wife, let us practice Christian contentment and gratitude to him, rather than discontent and covetousness. And let us find our deepest satisfaction in knowing him, rather than looking for it in the gifts that he gives.

## GLORIFY GOD WITH YOUR BODY

Above all, remember the words of 1 Corinthians 6:13, "The body is . . . for the Lord." This really means that the pressure is off, because your body is not your own. Isn't that what it says in 1 Corinthians 6:19? Because you and your body are not your own, and because your body is the temple of the Holy Spirit, the pressure is off. You know what you're supposed to do with your body. You are to glorify God with your body. That's it. There are no options. There isn't a menu from which you can choose and say, "Click, I'll do that one today." The only thing that you can do with your body is what will honor and glorify God. If you have even a hint of a question about something, don't do it. Check with someone else, check with your mom or your dad, or your pastor or elders. Check with someone who can help you if there's even the slightest question.

Finally, 1 Corinthians 6:14 says that God will raise your body. This is significant, especially because we Christians don't always make the necessary connections. The reality is that it is *your* body that will be raised. You will not be raised with another body. It will be your body. Paul used this as a reason to be pure. You are united with Christ. He said that your bodies are members of Christ. He didn't say, "You are a member of Christ," but "your bodies are members of Christ." There is honor and dignity in your bodies. The point here is, "Do you want to commit sexual immorality and unite the members of Christ with a prostitute?" Not only is this sin a violation of yourself and another—it is a violation between yourself and God. There is purity in the sexual relationship of a husband and his wife. This relationship is to remain pure (Heb. 13:4). It is a relationship that pictures the purity of the relationship of Christ and his church. It is a pure thing to have a full sexual relationship in marriage. It is wrong to see such sexual expression in marriage as less spiritual. What is impure is any sexual activity outside of this relationship.

You cannot expect to live a life with no temptations. But you must say no to all temptation and yes to God. In 1 Corinthians 6:18, Paul put it simply: "Flee from sexual immorality." You can't be sexually immoral if you're not there! Joseph is an incredible example. Joseph fled, quite possibly *completely naked,* rather than defile himself and deny God. You can flee any temptation because God said in 1 Corinthians 10:13 that "no temptation has seized you except what is common to man. And God is faithful; he will not let you be tempted beyond what you can bear. But when you are tempted, he will also provide a way out so that you can stand up under it." God will always provide a way of escape.

Sex isn't primarily biological. Sex is primarily spiritual. It is by definition a union, and that's what Paul said here when he spoke of sex as a union that takes place, using the language of marriage *even with a prostitute.* He referred to Genesis 2, with the language of marriage, to show how serious this is. In a marriage, the two become one flesh. If we seriously stopped to consider this, there would be less sexual immorality. What Paul is referring to here is the utter inappropriateness of such immoral behavior. Since this is the act of union between a husband and wife, it makes no sense whatsoever to apply it outside of marriage. He wants participants in such sinful behavior to know that their sin has draconian consequences, be it upon themselves, their families, their community, or in some instances even their nation. Marriage, with its physical expression, is a mystical union. It is the picture of the union of Christ and his church, who are one. This is why the warning against sexual sin cannot be overstated. This is why the temptations surrounding it are so severe. Even those who we think are the best of God's men and women are not exempt from danger here.

It is my hope that these warnings will keep many young lives, and many marriages and families, from being shipwrecked. Although alcohol, drugs, and gambling kill marriages and families, nothing so utterly destroys like sexual immorality. But even here, the God who will raise your body from the grave will make you pure, so that if you are truly repentant, even if your sin has been a terrible immorality, God will forgive you completely. But you must turn from it, and you must live a pure and righteous life. You must determine that no reason you gave yourself for doing what you did is a good enough reason for so dishonoring God, your body, and if you are married, your husband or your wife. Your life is to be pure and sanctified and never going in the direction of immorality. God judged Israel because he said she was an adulteress to him, her husband. That is the reason given. God wants you to be a holy and spotless bride, a pure people, a chaste people, allowing no immorality in the body. I promise you this, when you look back on it, you will never be able to say it was worth being sexually immoral. Don't forget it. You have to live with yourself after you've committed a sexually immoral offense. God wants you to live in purity. That is the only standard, for the Corinthian church, and for you.

**M**arriage is under fire more than any institution in our culture, with 50 percent of all marriages ending in divorce. Is there hope for marriage? There certainly is as far as the Bible is concerned. In Genesis, God said that it is not good for the man to be alone, and so he created a helper suitable for him (Gen. 2:18). Adam, seeing his helper, was ecstatic! His exclamation of delight is unfortunately left out of the translations. In every way, God blessed the institution of marriage. Paul, in 1 Timothy 3:2, went so far as to say that the officers of the church must be married men, and not simply married, but completely devoted to their wives. He called them "one-woman men." Yet here in 1 Corinthians 7, the controversy is confusing, for Paul said that it is good for a man not to marry. How are we to resolve this issue? And the church had better resolve it, because Christians seem to live as if it is better not to marry. Do they have apostolic sanction for this attitude? Is marriage good or is it an evil? Don't think that the answer is readily apparent. Many people

### 1 CORINTHIANS 7:1–7

¹Now for the matters you wrote about: It is good for a man not to marry. ²But since there is so much immorality, each man should have his own wife, and each woman her own husband. ³The husband should fulfill his marital duty to his wife, and likewise the wife to her husband. ⁴The wife's body does not belong to her alone but also to her husband. In the same way, the husband's body does not belong to him alone but also to his wife. ⁵Do not deprive each other except by mutual consent and for a time, so that you may devote yourselves to prayer. Then come together again so that Satan will not tempt you because of your lack of self-control. ⁶I say this as a concession, not as a command. ⁷I wish that all men were as I am. But each man has his own gift from God; one has this gift, another has that.

who have had miserable experiences in marriage would be quick to call it a great evil. We also have to ask if Paul is contradicting Moses, who wrote the passages in Genesis that refer to God's provision of marriage. Even closer to home, is Paul contradicting himself and his high view of marriage espoused in 1 Timothy 3 and 4?

We notice that 1 Corinthians 7 opened with Paul answering questions from the Corinthians. He said, "Now for the matters you wrote about . . ." What a series of perplexing questions they were! This first group of questions in 1 Corinthians 7 have to do with marriage, an issue with which the Corinthians had tremendous problems. In 1 Corinthians 8

Paul is confronted with the question of what to do about foods sacrificed to idols. In 1 Corinthians 12 the subject is spiritual gifts. As you can see, the Corinthians had many problems but also many important questions. Here the questions concern marriage, and Paul's answer is controversial, to say the least. If he is saying that it is morally *good* not to be married, then do we conclude that it is morally *bad* to be married, which is what many of the church fathers have taught?

I want to first rest our minds regarding the impossibility of contradiction. Though Paul wrote in 1 Timothy 4:1–3 that forbidding marriage would be a sign of end-time apostasy, here he is not contradicting himself or Moses. That is because his desire is not to keep men and women from marriage but to keep them from *immorality*. The word here in 1 Corinthians 7:1 that is translated "marry" is a synonym for sexual intercourse, and it is used as such in three other places in the Septuagint (the Greek Old Testament). For those who know God and his plan for life, there is no place for sex outside of marriage. Therefore the two concepts belong together, and the words become interchangeable. A marriage is a complete union of a man and wife, including a sexual relationship, and it is the only relationship with a legitimate sexual aspect. In Genesis 20:6, when God spoke to Abimelech in a dream before he *touched* Sarah, this is the word used. He would have taken her as his wife, and because she was married to Abraham, it would have been a violation against God. God spared Abimelech from this grave sin because he was innocent, unaware that Sarah was married. In Proverbs 6:29 we read the warning to men being tempted, "So is he who *sleeps* with another man's wife; no one who *touches* her will go unpunished." In Ruth 2:9 Boaz ordered his men not to *touch* Ruth. The context is clear. He was speaking against anyone harming her sexually. Therefore when Paul said, "It is good for a man not to marry," he was saying, "It is good for a man not to be involved in *sexual immorality.*"

Paul did not see marriage as a second-rate condition that was necessary to combat immorality! Rather, as the Scriptures state emphatically, marriage is very good (Gen. 2). A man cannot even be an elder if he is not married (1 Tim. 3:2, 5; Titus 1:6). In other words, if the *leaders* of the church should be married, it must be a good thing to be married. It is *never good* for a man to have a sexual relationship with a woman outside of marriage, because it is *very good* inside of marriage. The idea is not, "Because of sexual immorality, get married," as much as, "In the face of all this sexual immorality, remember that each of you should be having a sexually intimate relationship within marriage." "Each man having his own wife" means, "Each man having this special sexual relationship only with his wife." This, friends, is very different from thinking that this passage teaches that marriage is not good!

Since this is the case, and the dangers of sexual immorality are so prominent, the importance of having a good sexual relationship with your wife and no one else was in the forefront of Paul's thinking. He went on to elaborate on the responsibilities involved in a good sexual relationship in marriage. The English translation uses the term "marital duty," and though it sounds strange to us at this time, we all know he is referring to sexual responsibility in marriage. This indicates reciprocity—a mutual exchange of privileges and responsibilities. Notice what Paul did. He crushed the idea of sexual promiscuity, the idea of having as many sexual partners as you please. But he also crushed the idea of a lackluster sex life within marriage, because the Scriptures, in condemning immoral sex, never condemn marital sex! In fact, on the contrary, Paul argued *for* it. Here is what is the most interesting aspect of the whole exhortation. When you read this carefully, you see that Paul's pastoral concerns here show him to be two thousand years ahead of himself. He avoids all the modern evils and promotes the good. I'll demonstrate this by going through the responsibilities enjoined by Paul in these verses.

1. Men must never even think about getting involved in a sexually immoral relationship.
2. In the face of all the sexual pressures around you, all the immorality swirling by, it is imperative that you have a good sexual relationship with your spouse.
3. Neither the husband nor the wife should ever deprive each other of sexual enjoyment in their marriage.
4. Neither the husband nor the wife has rights over his or her body that would keep them from giving themselves to their spouse in sexual intimacy.
5. The body of the husband belongs to his wife, and the body of the wife belongs to her husband. Once again, there is reciprocity in this area of marriage.
6. The only time of sexual abstinence mentioned in the New Testament is here, and it is during short times devoted to prayer and fasting. (In the Old Testament there is also the time of a wife's monthly period and the time following the birth of her children.)
7. Following a time apart because of prayer and fasting, you are to come together again sexually.
8. You are to be careful about satanic temptation in this area. Specifically, you need to come together sexually

after a time apart for prayer, or you may be faced with a lack of self-control, which you then could live out by getting involved in sexual immorality. Paul's point is that people need to be aware that prayer, fasting, and sex don't go together. His idea was that you should put sex aside when you have a vital concern for which you need to pray. But even this was not a command . . . only his understanding of reality. His wish that all men were as he is did not mean that he wished all men were celibate *but that all men had self-control,* so that they could respect the fact that a sexual relationship, even in marriage, has bounds. He desired that they would not be so ill-equipped as to be tempted into sexual immorality during times of abstinence, because of a lack of self-control. At the same time he recognized that his self-control (*not his celibacy*) was a gift, and he recognized that while he had this gift . . . others had other gifts. (This was not marriage he was referring to here, because the institution of marriage isn't a gift someone has. It is the normative institution of our society. Of course this doesn't mean that your wife or your husband isn't a gift!)

What is also interesting is the timeless quality of Paul's instruction to the Corinthians, which leaves us with several very important lessons from these verses.

1. The first lesson comes through an explanation. Most commentators say that Paul concedes to allow marriage instead of commanding celibacy, that he concedes a lesser path for some, even though celibacy is

the better path, of which he has this special gift. I have already presented my interpretation, which is substantially different from that of my fellow Christian theologians. At the same time, a word of explanation may be of further assistance. From the days of the Fathers, marriage has often not been seen as a high calling. Jerome wrote, "If it is good not to marry, then it is bad to marry." It was not long before thinking such as this led to celibacy in the priesthood of the Roman Catholic Church. Commentators sometimes use Jesus as a proponent of celibacy because he said there are eunuchs for the kingdom of God. But remember, in that passage in Matthew 19, he did not say that his celibacy was a better path or that all should enter it. He just said it was a fact. If Paul in any way even suggested that celibacy is a higher calling or state, he was going against the creation account, in which we are told that it is not good for the man to be alone (period). If some are alone because they never found a spouse, or they are alone because they chose it, the fact is, according to the Scriptures, it is not good. Thus I believe that of the two, celibacy versus marriage, the obviously higher calling is marriage, because it is "good," and that while celibacy may happen, or may even be chosen, it is not the higher state.

2. This passage deals with being physically available for one's spouse, sexually. This conveys a sense of concern for each other sexually, with each partner giving his or her body to the other and doing all that they can to bring pleasure to the spouse. The idea is not, "Your body belongs to me. I can do with it what I want."

Not at all! Rather, you are to do all that you can to bring pleasure to your spouse.

3. All that you do with your spouse must be undergirded by love for the other person's well-being. That means you will never do anything your spouse doesn't want you to do. You will never do anything that will harm or shame your spouse. Your spouse is not an object. She is a person with needs and sensitivities that are meant to be respected.

4. The necessity for self-control is not in these circumstances a command for abstinence. Self-control is necessary for believers who are apart for a time of prayer. Self-control is necessary for believers who live in an environment that oozes sex and has no respect for marriage and the family.

5. If you are courting a person to whom you do not believe you will ever desire to give yourself, then you should not marry that person, because marriage is meant to be filled with sexual intimacy. Many marriages are filled instead with excuses and downright indifference sexually, so that even when there is no prayer, there is still no intimacy. If you are of marrying age and people tell you that it doesn't matter if you are attracted to the person you are considering marrying, they are wrong. I am not at all saying that this is *all* that matters, or even the most important of the things that matter, just that it *does* matter, because you are going to live an intimate life with that person. If the person is repulsive to you, it is wrong to enter into that relationship. Eventually this person will realize your abhorrence of him or her and be devastated by it.

6. Notice the cutting edge of these Scriptures, which are given by a man who many call a chauvinist. These are some of the most sensitive writings in the area of sexuality I have ever read. Remember that this was written almost two thousand years ago, to a world that hardly acknowledged the humanity of women. But the Scriptures did, and Jesus always did, and now, coming to the subject of sexual intimacy in marriage, the Scriptures recognize something else. They recognize the sexuality of the woman as well as that of the man. The Bible is not calling for a marriage in which a woman is told to be a sexual object for her husband. Instead, it calls for a profound mutual appreciation of the sexuality of each other.

7. This passage takes note of the priority of prayer. A marriage is not built on the sexual relationship. It is built on Christ. This text fully appreciates that when it calls a husband and wife to a life of prayer and teaches them that prayer comes first.

8. There is to be no deprivation of each other. I will say here that in my counseling, most often it is a husband who reports that his wife is not as interested sexually as he would like her to be, although I hear the other side as well. I would like to call attention to the fact that often this withholding of a wife has to do with the way a husband goes about things. For example, the injunction to not withhold yourself doesn't mean that a husband can demand sex whenever he wants. This approach is guaranteed to fail, because even if your wife is willing to be completely passive to your sexual activity, I hope *this* isn't what you want. This is what the

passage is addressing in terms of learning how to please the *other*—understanding differences in God's creation and learning what pleases her. It works both ways. A good sexual relationship flows out of a good personal relationship. This doesn't mean that there are no problems, but that you are willing to work hard at solving problems together, and not let them be brushed under the rug. Then you can expect to go to bed and have a great, loving, sexual experience.

All of this presupposes a commitment to Jesus Christ. We are talking about loving each other in marriage, not simply having a sexual relationship with each other, and love comes from God. Our lives, our families, and our marriages depend upon us knowing the love of God. We are not capable of giving this kind of care, nurture, and self-sacrifice on our own. We must be empowered by the love of God. We must see how Christ loves his bride and then love one another. Through all of life's struggles, God wants you to have enjoyment. He wants you to be blessed. He places you in a world addicted to sex, enslaved by perversion, and yet he doesn't leave you gawking senselessly. He gives you marriage, a husband, and a wife, and says, "Go and enjoy. Amidst life's many responsibilities, enjoy." Song of Songs speaks of love,

> Place me like a seal over your heart,
>     like a seal on your arm;
> for love is as strong as death. . . .
> It burns like blazing fire,
>     like a mighty flame.
> Many waters cannot quench love;
>     rivers cannot wash it away.

If one were to give
    all the wealth of his house for love,
    it would be utterly scorned. (Song 8:6–7)

True love can't be manipulated, paid for, demanded, or anything else. But when you love each other in a Christ-like way, love will blossom, and your love life will be a delight! No, this is not a passage about celibacy. It is a passage about love!

**T**here is nothing nobler or more admirable than when two people who see eye to eye keep house as man and wife, confounding their enemies and delighting their friends" (Homer, c. 700 B.C.). There can be no greater blessing on earth than that blessing enjoyed within the institution of marriage. Yet there can be no greater misery than that misery experienced within the same institution. That is because two people, both sinners from birth, inherently self-oriented, live together in the deepest union possible, a union that can thrive only when each individual is prepared to die to self and live for God daily. The Corinthians had written to Paul about several problems that they faced in their marriages that were difficult for them to resolve.

Corinth was a hub of sexual promiscuity. Even in the church this had an impact, because some said that it didn't matter what you did with your body, as long as you served the Lord with your heart. Paul corrected that when he said, "Flee from sexual immorality. All other sins a man commits are out-

### 1 CORINTHIANS 7:8-16

⁸Now to the unmarried and the widows I say: It is good for them to stay unmarried, as I am. ⁹But if they cannot control themselves, they should marry, for it is better to marry than to burn with passion.

¹⁰To the married I give this command (not I, but the Lord): A wife must not separate from her husband. ¹¹But if she does, she must remain unmarried or else be reconciled to her husband. And a husband must not divorce his wife.

¹²To the rest I say this (I, not the Lord): If any brother has a wife who is not a believer and she is willing

side his body, but he who sins sexually sins against his own body. Do you not know that your body is a temple of the Holy Spirit, who is in you, whom you have received from God? You are not your own; you were bought with a price. Therefore honor God with your body" (1 Cor. 6:18–20). At the same time that Paul was teaching the dignity of the body and the sanctity of marriage, a sect developed that was also popular in Corinth. These individuals promoted celibacy. They said that celibacy was the highest form of spirituality, and this idea even worked its way into the church, so that husbands and wives stopped having sexual relations together. Paul had to correct that error, so that spouses knew that in marriage they had a responsibility to each other. He taught them that the sexual relationship in the marriage bond is very good. They shouldn't deprive each other sexually, especially since this could lead to satanic temptations and even sexual immorality. These were to live with him, he must not divorce her. [13]And if a woman has a husband who is not a believer and he is willing to live with her, she must not divorce him. [14]For the unbelieving husband has been sanctified through his wife, and the unbelieving wife has been sanctified through her believing husband. Otherwise your children would be unclean, but as it is, they are holy.

[15]But if the unbeliever leaves, let him do so. A believing man or woman is not bound in such circumstances; God has called us to live in peace. [16]How do you know, wife, whether you will save your husband? Or, how do you know, husband, whether you will save your wife?

his concerns for married people in the church, and we explored them in depth in the last chapter. But these concerns did not include everyone in the church.

Further questions emerged. Some of them are found in 1 Corinthians 7:8–16, where Paul dealt with those who were unmarried and widows and those who were married and wanted to divorce. When we scrutinize the problems of Corinth, it is as if we are putting our culture under a microscope. There is nothing new under the sun. Marriage and sexual problems are not new. Before the Word of Christ came to Corinth, all manner of problems existed. Divorce proliferated. Under these circumstances, it is easy to comprehend how some of the people chose celibacy. Paul didn't condemn that, but he made it clear that celibacy is not to be the norm for God's people. Rather, they should learn how to live together and love each other in marriage, view the marriage bond as a lifetime covenant, and treat each other with complete dignity and respect as persons created in the image of God.

### UNMARRIED MEN AND WIDOWS

Paul began with instructions to the "unmarried and the widows." The group that he refers to as widows is clear. These were women who had lost their husbands through death. But who were those whom he referred to as unmarried? Were they individuals who were never married, or were they people who were unmarried at the time but had been previously married? Or were there people in both categories? This word *unmarried* is used three other times in the Scriptures, all of them in this same passage, and speaks of those who had been previously married. John MacArthur said, "The term unmarried indicates those who were previously married, but are now widowed, people who are now single . . . therefore . . . divorced."[1] We know they were not single as the result of the death of a spouse, because they were not called widowers. These previously married but now divorced men, and widows, were asking whether it was all right for them to be remarried. How did Paul handle this?

Paul put them in the same category as himself (1 Cor. 7:8). What can this mean? I think it can mean only one thing—he was a man who was previously married. Why else would he include himself in a group of previously married men and women? Why else would he suggest that these previously married individuals remain as he was? But this is not the

---

1. John Mac Arthur, *The MacArthur New Testament Commentary, 1 Corinthians* (Chicago: Moody, 1984), 163.

only reason to believe he was married. He had been a member of the Sanhedrin, and to be an elder in this capacity a man had to be at least thirty years of age and married. What would this mean? Either he was a widower, or else he was divorced. The latter situation seems more valid to me. We can say only that if this assumption is accurate, there is no biblical mention of it. Perhaps when Paul was converted, his wife left him. I say this because it is clear from his teaching that he would not divorce his wife. He said, "A husband is not to divorce his wife." It is also possible that Paul's wife had died, but in that case, one would expect some loving reference to her, of which there is none. We would also *probably* see some encouragement for remarriage, whereas instead he suggested that the formerly married should remain unmarried as he was. It is also possible that Paul was never married. Though I grant that possibility, contrary to what is sometimes said about Paul, his writings show a sensitivity to women that seems marked by experience, which I elaborated on in the last chapter. If you ask why his wife would divorce him if he was such a sensitive man, I can only say that I don't know. His zeal for Christ could have been repulsive to her, and the pressures to leave such a man could have been considerable in Jewish circles.

Paul's next directive is in 1 Corinthians 7:9. Here the command is given (the present active infinitive indicates a command, not just a concession) to allow marriage to another group of formerly married Christians. The reason is clear: they cannot be expected to serve the Lord faithfully if they are consumed with the desire to be married so they can share life together and have a sexual relationship with each other. But now another question arises. If these are formerly divorced men, how can Paul command marriage to them? (Of course there is

no problem with the widows.) How can he command divorced men to remarry? Is it to guard them against sexual immorality? That would be pretty horrible for the woman, if that
were all that he intended. But it isn't. For an individual who
must live in a sexual environment but cannot be celibate, he
must remarry. He must prepare himself for married life so that
he is not using a woman as a means to keep himself from immorality. His devotion and affection are presupposed. If such
affection were absent, she would become someone's wife just
so that he didn't commit fornication with other women. If a
husband were that kind of a man, you could never be sure
about him anyway. Rather (I reiterate this), as I explained in
the last chapter, marriage is a relationship of love and respect
for each other. People are not to get married to have their own
sex object.

But even that still doesn't answer how Paul could have
commanded this, if these men were divorced. The answer here
is that these men were not *morally at fault* in these divorces. I
think that point becomes clear from his statement that if they
are as he is, then they were men whose wives left them *after
their conversions.* At this point remember: If a person is not responsible for the divorce, he or she can remarry with the
Lord's blessing. The couple alone should not make that decision. The church leaders should be involved with the couple,
and the innocent party should be officially vindicated.

## Married Couples

Paul's next instruction is aimed at the married. He said, "A
wife must not separate from her husband. But if she does, she
must remain unmarried or else be reconciled to her husband."

The same basic guidance is given to the husband. Many people have used this to justify separation, that is, remaining married but in an *unreconciled* state and living in different places. Often counselors and therapists, even Christians, will recommend a trial separation. The use of this word *separate* in our text does not mean in the least that the Bible condones or permits such a separation. As you can see from the text, the separation spoken of in 1 Corinthians 7:10 leaves a person *unmarried* in verse 11. Thus, this separation is another synonym for divorce, or else they wouldn't be unmarried by virtue of it. As Paul said in 1 Corinthians 7:11, if a woman does divorce her husband (for *any* unbiblical reason) she *cannot* remarry, and the same would hold true for the man. In other words, men and women are not allowed to divorce at will. In fact, the only reason given by Jesus is sexual immorality, and the term is far more inclusive than most people would ever care to admit.

Paul exposited that statement of Jesus in the latter part of the chapter. He provided a framework to understand its full implications. Paul was so concerned to correct illegitimate divorces that he said if you secure such a divorce, you can still be reconciled afterwards. One of the questions I hear is this, "Can a couple be reconciled after divorcing?" The answer is given by Paul, "Yes, and they will be married again." Two people can be divorced and then forgiven by each other, which often brings about a remarriage but does not necessarily do so. For example, if a husband is unfaithful to his wife, gets AIDS, and repents, she must forgive him, but she doesn't have to be married to him. If a relative abuses a child and asks forgiveness, you must grant it, but you never *ever* have to see that relative again. You must not hold bitterness, because that would destroy *you*, but you do not have to enter into a relationship with that person again. You can also expect the full force of the legal system to act against that individual, no matter how closely they were related to the child they harmed.

### MIXED MARRIAGES

In 1 Corinthians 7:12, another group was added. These were "the rest" of the people in the church who were married but not covered in the situations Paul had already mentioned. These people were in mixed marriages, that is, a believer with an unbeliever. How did this come about? In our day it happens all the time when a believer marries an unbeliever. This is completely against the will and the Word of God. Yet it happens. This was not the situation in Corinth, which was a place where the gospel was proclaimed for the first time and a number of people came to faith in Christ. They were told by some that if they wanted to be *really* holy, they had to divorce their unbelieving spouses. Paul had a ready answer to that: No! If the unbelieving spouse wants to live with the believing spouse, then the believer should accept that and remain in the marriage. When they are together, the unbelieving spouse is sanctified, as well as the children.

Yet another situation emerged, in which the unbelieving spouse in a mixed marriage wanted to divorce the believing spouse. Many of those who were believers became frantic to remain married with this unbeliever who wanted a divorce. What were they to do? Again Paul had an answer. It was that the believing spouse was to let the unbelieving spouse secure the divorce and not fight against him or her. They were afraid that as believers they would be forced to remain unmarried and never be allowed to remarry again. This would mean that they would, in effect, be punished for the sin of their spouse. But Paul put this to rest quickly, when he said they were "not bound . . . God has called us to live in peace" (1 Cor. 7:15).

Although Paul gave very specific directives with far-reaching implications for the believer and unbeliever, at the same time he seemed to be bold one moment as he said, "I say, not the Lord" (1 Cor. 7:12), and then hesitant in the next, "I say this, not I, but the Lord" (v. 10). What did he mean? Was he thinking out loud? Was he in danger of adding his own thoughts and missing the Lord in all of these instructions?

This is how Paul is often critiqued—that he was offering opinions and thoughts. I want to be the first to say to you, without any hesitation or equivocation, that Paul's seeming hesitation is a mark *not* of his limitation but of his office as an apostle. He demonstrated that in four places in this chapter: "Not I, but the Lord" (v. 10), "I say, not the Lord" (v. 12), "I have no command from the Lord, but I give a judgment" (v. 25), "In my judgment, . . . and I think that I too have the Spirit of God" (v. 40). What he was saying in these four places was not, "I am now about to give you uninspired opinion." Not at all! What he was saying in verse 10, for example is that the directive is not his but the Lord's. For example, the Lord himself gave this instruction in Mark, "What God has joined together, let man not separate" (Mark 10:9), and in verse 12 Paul was elucidating on what the Lord had said. The specifics of what the Spirit of God was giving Paul were not found in any of the Gospels, because they were a further application of old principles. He was not calling this human opinion. In the earlier chapter on sexual sin, at one point I expressed an opinion. Specifically, I said it was "my opinion" that sexual enslavement is worse than drug or alcohol addiction. That is different from Paul, who was saying that his conclusion is not human opinion but additional revelation!

Let me put it another way. He was saying that sometimes he quoted Christ and other times he didn't, and in these other times, he was giving new revelation. Paul's concluding argument was to affirm that he too had the Spirit of God (v. 40). It is not just the other apostles, and it is certainly not those who would promote promiscuity or celibacy. They were not the ones who had the Spirit of God. He too, like the other apostles and the Lord, had the Spirit of God in these matters. It is important to remember that everything Paul said in his life, even after conversion, was not infallible. There were times when he could be wrong. But whenever he wrote Scripture, he was an infallible spokesman for God. When you try to understand Paul, you must first understand that you are dealing with an inspired writer of the Word of God, whose words are true. We may fail in our attempt to understand them. We may even become foolish if we suggest that we have divine understanding of all of them. Indeed, I can change my mind, even about my understanding of something in this very chapter. Paul's words though, will never change, because his word is nothing less than, and nothing *else* than, the Word of God.

## INSTRUCTION FOR TODAY

Paul's instruction is of immense help to the church, even two thousand years later. The teaching of Paul was never abstract or unearthly. It was point after point of incisive, relevant instruction. It was written to help the church through one very difficult problem after another.

1. *Directives for divorce.* I speak with people who tell me of marriages that they describe as terrible . . . marriages from which they want to escape! They assume that because the marriage is so bad and our society's laws are so lenient, that God doesn't disapprove of their divorcing. The Scriptures give clear guidance in this area. There is no biblical ground for divorce, except sexual immorality and desertion, which Paul raises at the end of this chapter. Because of this, there should be real concern to be careful before you enter into a marriage. Make sure that you are not just marrying someone because he has asked you. Make sure you are not just marrying someone because you are bored with being single, or as some people have told me, are tired of the singles scene.

   But what about those who find themselves in a difficult marriage because of a poor youthful decision, or because of unexpected changes later on in life? That is the time to trust in God. It is God who takes care of us in life. It is God who measures our challenges and gives us only what we can bear. It is God who plans our lives because he said, " 'For I know the plans I have for you,' declares the LORD, 'plans to prosper you and not to harm you, plans to give you hope and a future' " (Jer. 29:11). It is God who wants to teach us and show us new truths in life. He has given us the resources of the rest of the church body, and he has given us prayer, which he assures us he will always answer. It is God who will use our lives to bless the whole body of Christ, which is what we learn from reading about the ordinary, struggling believers in the Scriptures, who even now encourage us, thousands of years later!

2. *Directives for marriage.* Paul showed what happens when a believer marries an unbeliever. There are all kinds of troubles. The most common difficulty that I have seen is when the believer hopes that the unbeliever will change and become a believer. Instead, the believer is changed by the unbeliever. Slowly but surely, he or she gives up standing for the faith and eventually has nothing left. I have seen believers deeply in love with unbelievers, just "knowing" that everything will work out. I have seen their heartbreak later, in the deep and powerful loneliness they experience, having no real communion with a spouse. Why? Because the spouse lives only for this world, while the believer lives for Christ.

I have seen believers seduced and lied to by unbelievers who said they were Christians just to win the other person. This is one of the reasons that even though there are enormous sexual pressures against which they contend, I tell young people to wait and work on their friendship with a potential spouse. That way they know (*in advance*) whether their relationship can stand the test of time and challenge, before they enter into an indissoluble union from which they can never extricate themselves. I received a letter from someone who said she wished she were dead because her despair in her marriage was so great. Be very careful, for Paul said clearly, "Do not be yoked with unbelievers" (2 Cor. 6:14).

Peter also addressed women who are in marriages with unbelievers and gave them direction. He told them to be like Sarah, Abraham's wife, to respect their husbands and have no fear. God took care of Sarah and answered her prayers. Peter also admonished women to cultivate their inner beauty, which is precious to God. Though they could not interact spiritually with a husband, they were in a continual spiritual interaction with God!

3. *Directives for previously married believers.* There is nothing wrong with being single. You have been married. If you have been widowed, you have experienced joys in marriage and the sadness of the death of your beloved. If you are divorced, you have experienced bitterness, especially if you are innocent. You are not forced to remarry. You already know how much work it takes to make a marriage succeed. Now, being single, you can give yourself single-mindedly to the work of the church. The Scriptures encourage you to think about this.

4. *Directives for those in marriages with unbelievers.* In every church there are some people in this situation. There are also some who are contemplating entering this situation, and they cannot believe that it will be hard for *them.* If you are in such a situation, you must learn to be at peace and content in that relationship, entrusting your unbelieving husband or wife to the Lord and loving that spouse, even though he may think that your faith is foolish. Your faith isn't foolish. Your faith is precious.

One day you will see that your patience and endurance have real rewards and blessings. Right now, it seems like so much pain, but one day you will see the bigger picture that God had in mind. Only remember this, do not lose heart. Do not give up. Do not run away from an unbelieving spouse who will continue to live with you. Make the best of it; in fact, make the most of it. Be a good husband. Be a good wife. Trust that God will bless all that you do. Remember the promise that is given to you that the unbelieving spouse is sanctified through the believing spouse (1 Cor. 7:14). It is an incredible promise that the unbelieving spouse experiences God's blessings to the believer, though it is not salvation that is promised. This is also why you must not leave a spouse who will live with you. As difficult as it is for you, it is also difficult for him. Because of this willingness to stay under real spiritual pressure, the blessing of God touches him so powerfully that he is sanctified. The moral and spiritual influence of your life as a believer will create an indelible imprint on your unbelieving spouse. Don't give up! This also shows how powerful the marriage bond is. The two become one, and the blessings of the one are experienced by the other.

5. *Directives for those in marriages with unbelievers who have children.* This directive is inextricably connected with the one above. The believer is so often afraid of being defiled by the unbeliever, especially when the unbeliever has an obviously unchristian lifestyle. But in the situation where your spouse will live with you and you exercise strength in the Lord, your strength will bring blessing to the husband.

Another fear has to do with the children. Specifically, will they be lost, and will they be destroyed spiritually by the unbelieving parent? Paul's answer is no. The children experience the sanctifying influence of a believing parent. I remember dealing with a family that had a believing parent, an unbelieving parent, and several very young children. The unbelieving parent tried to influence his young children not to believe, but each child grew up trusting in Christ. Each child prayed and hoped for the unbelieving parent to believe. I remember the day that this parent came to faith in Christ. It was a thrill to the entire family, as well as everyone who had prayed for this person over the years. Every family with an unbelieving parent or child can know that God is at work, and when they entrust that husband, wife, or child to God, God will be merciful and perhaps even bring salvation.

6. *Directives concerning the salvation of the unbelieving spouse.* In 1 Corinthians 7:16 you are called to stay with an unbelieving spouse who is willing to continue in the marriage. It also gives the reason, "How do you know, wife, whether you will save your husband? How do you know, husband, whether you will save your wife?" Your efforts may bring about the salvation of your unbelieving spouse, which would be the most wonderful thing imaginable. So don't give up. You don't know how God will use your efforts.

7. *Directives for remarriage.* Anyone who is declared by the church the innocent party in a divorce is free to remarry. People who had a spouse who committed adultery or abandoned them, refusing to live with them, is free. Once the church has declared the guilty individual to be a heathen and the state has declared them di-

vorced, they may enter into a new marriage before God. If one of the parties was at one time immoral, but that was forgiven and the innocent party was willing *at that time* to reconcile, they cannot use that as an option for divorce *later on*. Likewise, when an innocent party reconciles and later commits adultery or deserts a spouse, the formerly guilty party is now innocent and not under bondage. This person is free to remarry, because the former sins have been blotted out and cannot be held against the person ever again.

These are significant directives. I hope that every Christian takes these seriously, so that every marriage will be one that is enjoyed by two believing spouses, and every family filled with believing children. There is little grief that is worse than the experience of unbelief in the family. There is very little that breaks parents' hearts more than an unbelieving child, especially when a parent knows how sinful they (the parents) have been and how easily they may have done things they perceive as contributing to the unbelief of their child. Indeed there can be guilt, but this passage is not meant to fill the hearts of spouses and parents with doom and sorrow but rather with hope. It is the hope that our sovereign God will protect his people, that he will guard his covenant children, and that he will work to the salvation of unbelieving spouses. Life is not easy. This has never been an easy subject on which to teach. Everywhere in the church of Christ, there is grief for lost husbands and wives and children. They are not lost to God. He knows them. He watches over them. He hears your prayers. He answers them. So don't grow weary in your labors. I am convinced that many who now sow in tears will one day reap with joy!

# 11

There was a man who was being interviewed for a Christian newspaper by a group of believers who sat around drinking coffee and smoking cigarettes, cigars, and pipes. Each in turn offered him something. But the smoke made him sick, so he didn't want to smoke with them. They asked him, "Don't you believe in Christian liberty?" He responded that he thought his Christian liberty allowed him not to do things if he chose. Though he didn't see *their* activity as sin, they accused him of being a legalist and not believing in Christian liberty. What does Christian liberty allow, and what is the gracious Christian way to interact?

This chapter is all about Christian liberty. It is a subject that has caused much controversy in the church throughout its history. In Corinth, a threatening problem emerged early in the life of the church. It was the issue of whether it was right to eat the meats that were offered to idols.

Because Corinth was a city filled with idolatry, those who came to Christ had previously been involved with that very

### 1 CORINTHIANS 8

[1]Now about food sacrificed to idols: We know that we all possess knowledge. Knowledge puffs up, but love builds up. [2]The man who thinks he knows something does not yet know as he ought to know. [3]But the man who loves God is known by God.

[4]So then, about eating food sacrificed to idols: We know that an idol is nothing at all in the world and that there is no God but one. [5]For even if there are so-called gods, whether in heaven or on earth (as indeed there are many "gods" and many "lords"), [6]yet for us there is but one God, the Father, from whom all things came and for whom we live; and there is but one Lord, Jesus Christ, through whom all things came and through whom we live.

[7]But not everyone knows this. Some people are still

idolatry. New believers clearly understood that idol worship was an abomination to God, and they condemned that entire system of false religion—the entire realm of idolatry. But in their city, pagan priests frequented the markets and sold the meats that had been used in their idol sacrifices. To put it bluntly, anyone could get a great deal on such meat.

Take yourself back to Corinth in those times. Here is the imaginary situation. You are enjoying an incredible feast of roast beef. One of the zealous new converts is devouring his dinner, just like everyone else. The conversation might have gone something like this, "Paul, this is great!" "Yeah, kid, this is really good roast beef." "I've never tasted anything like this,

> so accustomed to idols that when they eat such food they think of it as having been sacrificed to an idol, and since their conscience is weak, it is defiled. [8]But food does not bring us near to God; we are no worse if we do not eat, and no better if we do.
>
> [9]Be careful, however, that the exercise of your freedom does not become a stumbling block to the weak. [10]For if anyone with a weak conscience sees you who have this knowledge eating in an idol's temple, won't he be emboldened to eat what has been sacrificed to idols? [11]So this weak brother, for whom Christ died, is destroyed by your knowledge. [12]When you sin against your brothers in this way and wound their weak conscience, you sin against Christ. [13]Therefore, if what I eat causes my brother to fall into sin, I will never eat meat again, so that I will not cause him to fall.

Paul. Where'd ya get it?" "You know, down on Zeus Street, that shop on the corner. Well, they had a special on a side of beef that the old Olympian priest brought in. Good stuff, isn't it?" At that moment the new convert is confused and wondering, "How can this be? How can idolatry be evil, and it be okay for the apostle Paul to be eating meat offered to idols without a care in the world?"

Let me give you another example. In the neighborhood where I grew up as a Jewish boy, there were four butcher shops, three of which were kosher. The fourth was run by a Jewish man but wasn't kosher. Think of this—I was scared of any meat that was not kosher. I was scared that if I ate it, I would get really sick. But I was especially nervous about nonkosher meat sold by a Jewish butcher!

Now jump ahead. I came to faith in Christ. I was invited to someone's home and saw this big, beautiful roast put on the table. I was about to dig in . . . "Funny-looking chicken," I thought. But it smelled great, and it cut like butter. As the fork traveled to my mouth, I happened to ask, "What is this?" I was told, "Pork roast." What did I do? I felt a bit sick and excused myself momentarily from the table to pray about how to handle this diplomatically, because I was nauseated and bewildered. I wondered, "How can it be okay to eat this meat? God said this was unclean." In a nutshell, this is what the controversy in this chapter was all about. Though the ceremonial laws are no longer in effect for the Christian, there are those whose consciences are engrained with the Old Testament diet. Those whose consciences are freer are in danger of offending the more sensitive believers.

Paul talked about freedom in 1 Corinthians 8:9. What does this mean? What are its limits? What is Paul's argument? First of all, this freedom, as Paul said, is "your freedom." This is an exciting thought! This issue isn't just about meats. It is about *freedom*, and a very personal freedom at that, for it is your freedom. You are free to avoid the things that God condemns—to avoid what God finds detestable. You are also free to enjoy what he either commands or permits! Finally, you are free to decide what to do in areas where God has been silent. The best example of this is in the situation that Paul faced. Regarding the eating of meats offered to idols, Paul said, "You are free to eat." Paul also said, "You are free not to eat." In general, the limits of freedom are clear: you can't do what is prohibited. That is, you can't commit adultery. You can't steal.

You can't do things that God condemns, just because you are free. But you should be cautious with your freedom, because in the more subtle areas, you can't even do things you are allowed to do, if in the doing of these things, you would cause a brother to stumble. Be cautious, because love is a higher priority than freedom. If you love your brothers and sisters in Christ, then you will be careful not to do anything that would hurt them. They can be hurt because their sensitive consciences tell them something is wrong. When they see you do it, they may go against their consciences and do it anyway, which would be wrong for them.

I received a letter from someone who attended a conference at which I spoke. Listen to what he asked me: "Why am I continually being offered alcoholic beverages by Christians?" He was troubled by this. I believe that we often take our freedom and disgrace it by harming others who don't feel right exercising that same freedom. Why can't someone who is free in a certain area be content to be free, rather than try to have others do the same things he or she does? That isn't freedom. It is a manipulation that causes others to stumble, to sin. Many Christians have been asked, "Aren't you free?" in regard to alcohol. I have come to think that many believers who think they are strong are simply contemptuous of the sensitivities of many others in the body of Christ. They use their license as a cover for self-indulgence.

While Paul agreed with the argument of those who claimed Christian liberty, he was at odds with their application. They said that they could eat meats offered to idols without any hindrance, because they had knowledge. They *knew* that an idol is not God, because there is only one God and that is the Lord. Therefore idols are *nothing.* Thus they reasoned, "How could it possibly matter if you eat meat sacrificed to nothing?" Paul refuted this argument immediately, not because it was inaccurate but because it showed a complete lack of concern for the weaker person. His response showed this when he said, "But not everyone knows this. Some people are still so accustomed to idols that when they eat such food they think of it as having been sacrificed to an idol, and since their conscience is weak, it is defiled" (1 Cor. 8:7).

When I was teaching in Japan, I visited a Buddhist temple where I saw people strike a large gong. I learned that the purpose was to smack it hard enough for the sound to be heard by the gods. In fact, the people were so eager to communicate with their deity that they lined the walls of their temples with thousands of prayer requests. The problem is that there is no god who will answer them. I talked to the Buddhist priest and tried to explain to him that he gave his life for gods that were nothing.

Paul argued that if weaker believers feel *in some way* that a connection to an idol is offensive, then respect that, without making them feel foolish. It is not right to encourage someone to do something that his conscience tells him he shouldn't do. The conscience should be respected. There is a danger that ignoring one's conscience could lead to doing other things that are wrong, things that are not indifferent but are sin. There is a time, however, to educate his conscience and teach him which matters are definite and which matters can be decided by each individual.

Paul also said, "We know that we all possess knowledge" (1 Cor. 8:1). But then he attacked the application of that knowledge. These people were neglecting an important point. "Knowledge puffs up, but love builds up," Paul said. They understood about meat that was offered to idols but failed the test on pride. With their greater sense of freedom, they were proud rather than loving the brothers around them who were not comfortable with this practice. In the same way, people in our day might be proud of the freedom they possess without caring for the brothers around them. The Christian life isn't how much you know, or how strong you are, or how much Christian liberty you possess, but how much you love.

Paul's line of reasoning, while attacking a view of Christian freedom that was harming the weaker brethren, was at the same time silencing an incipient Gnosticism, a heresy that said you were saved by your knowledge. This heresy condemned those who did not possess knowledge. But Paul said, "We all possess knowledge." This slices through the elitist mentality that says only some have knowledge. But further, he showed that God esteems not knowledge but love, especially the love of God. "The man who loves God is known by God" (1 Cor. 8:3). If you have true knowledge, then you will undoubtedly love God. Then your highest goal will never be the enjoyment of your freedom at someone else's expense. You'll know that freedom without love is shallow and worthless. What should you do in a situation where the expression of your freedom may, as Paul said, hurt the conscience of a weak believer? Simple—you don't push the weaker brother to experience what you do. Rather, you limit your freedom.

The Corinthians had argued, "Food does not bring us near to God; we are no worse if we do not eat, and no better if we do" (1 Cor. 8:8). This is true. Alfalfa sprouts might be healthier than potato chips, but does God care about your diet, unless you are a glutton, or anorexic, or bulimic? Jesus said, "What goes into a man's mouth does not make him 'unclean,' but what comes out of his mouth, that is what makes him 'unclean' " (Matt. 15:11). They were right. God really doesn't care about foods. Even in the Old Testament, all of the food laws were designed to point out not primarily the uncleanness of a food but the uncleanness of the person. The goal of Leviticus was to cause a person to ask, "How can I ever possibly become clean?" This was to lead him to desire forgiveness from God. But though God is not concerned with the food you eat, he does care about your freedom becoming a snare to the weaker brother.

In the letter I had received from the young man I mentioned earlier, he wrote, "I turned twenty-one last December, and you know, it's funny. I've been offered more wine and beer by adult Christians than by non-Christians." He asked me what he should do about this. I said, "Benjamin, if you don't want to drink, you are free to never touch these substances. This is your Christian freedom. Don't let anyone manipulate you against this stance of your conscience."

Notice how emphatically Paul closed this section. "When you sin against your brothers in this way and wound their weak consciences, *you sin against Christ*" (1 Cor. 8:12). The warning is, "Be careful," because Christ's interest in the weaker brother is greater than his interest in you exercising your freedom. The consequences of disregarding the other brother will bring an offense against Christ, which he will not leave unsettled.

Paul summarized, "Therefore, if what I eat causes my brother to fall into sin, I will never eat meat again, so that I will not cause him to fall" (1 Cor. 8:13). A more literal translation would put it this way, even more forcefully, "Therefore if what I eat causes my brother to fall into sin, I will not eat meat again, as long as the world remains, so that I will not cause my brother to fall into sin."

These principles have a great practical impact for our lives.

1. You should always ask yourself, "Is what I am doing consistent with the Word of God and the will of God?" (James 4:15).
2. You should always ask yourself, "Is what I am doing profitable for me and for others?" (1 Cor. 6:12). This passage teaches that all things are lawful but not all are profitable.
3. You should always ask yourself, "Am I loving others or just being selfish?" (1 John 4:11). It is so easy to say, "This person is so messed up, I will never let his standard influence me." What we are saying is, "I love me and my pleasures so much that I will never let anything or anyone change them."
4. You should always ask, "Is what I am doing building others up or tearing them down?" (Eph. 4:29). It is so easy to have no concern for the building up of the church. Paul was willing to forego a pleasure in his life for the building up of the body of Christ. Paul's example was that even what is *allowable* is *disposable* for the sake of Christ!

**D**o not be idolaters" (1 Cor. 10:7). "Flee from idolatry" (1 Cor. 10:14). These exhortations were in response to the question of whether it was permissible to eat foods that were offered to idols. As we discussed in the last chapter, idols were nothing, and eating food offered to idols was a matter of indifference, but the consciences of people were not an indifferent matter. If people were caused to sin by others' freedom in eating food offered to idols, then they should never eat this food again!

In the city of Corinth, religious feasts, using food offered to idols, were celebrated with accompanying idolatry. Pressure was applied to the believers to attend these idolatrous religious services. Though idols were nothing, the idolatry connected with these feasts could destroy them spiritually, so they needed to avoid these celebrations at all costs. Paul gave them several examples from Israel's history to substantiate his concern.

The example in 1 Corinthians 10, which refers to Exodus 32:1–4, told the story about when Israel was delivered out of

### 1 CORINTHIANS 10

¹For I do not want you to be ignorant of the fact, brothers, that our forefathers were all under the cloud and that they all passed through the sea. ²They were all baptized into Moses in the cloud and in the sea. ³They all ate the same spiritual food ⁴and drank the same spiritual drink; for they drank from the spiritual rock that accompanied them, and that rock was Christ. ⁵Nevertheless, God was not pleased with most of them; their bodies were scattered over the desert.

⁶Now these things occurred as examples to keep us from setting our hearts on evil things as they did. ⁷Do not be idolaters, as some of them were; as it is written: "The people sat down to eat and drink and got up to indulge in pagan revelry." ⁸We should not commit sexual immorality, as some of them did—and in one day twenty-three thousand of them died. ⁹We should not test the Lord, as some of them did—and were killed by snakes. ¹⁰And do not grumble, as some of them did—and were killed by the destroying angel.

¹¹These things happened to them as examples and were written down as warnings for us, on whom the fulfillment of the ages has come. ¹²So, if you think you are standing firm, be careful that you don't fall! ¹³No temptation has seized you except what is common to man. And God is faithful; he will not let you be tempted beyond what you can bear. But when you are tempted, he will also provide a way out so that you can stand up under it.

[14]Therefore, my dear friends, flee from idolatry. [15]I speak to sensible people; judge for yourselves what I say. [16]Is not the cup of thanksgiving for which we give thanks a participation in the blood of Christ? And is not the bread that we break a participation in the body of Christ? [17]Because there is one loaf, we, who are many, are one body, for we all partake of the one loaf.

[18]Consider the people of Israel: Do not those who eat the sacrifices participate in the altar? [19]Do I mean then that a sacrifice offered to an idol is anything, or that an idol is anything? [20]No, but the sacrifices of pagans are offered to demons, not to God, and I do not want you to be participants with demons. [21]You cannot drink the cup of the Lord and the cup of demons too; you cannot have a part in both the Lord's table and the table of demons. [22]Are we trying to arouse the Lord's jealousy? Are we stronger than he?

[23]"Everything is permissible"—but not everything is beneficial. "Everything is permissible"—but not everything is constructive. [24]Nobody should seek his own good, but the good of others.

[25]Eat anything sold in the meat market without raising questions of conscience, [26]for, "The earth is the Lord's, and everything in it."

[27]If some unbeliever invites you to a meal and you want to go, eat whatever is put before you without raising questions of conscience. [28]But if anyone says to you, "This has been offered in sacrifice," then do not eat it, both for the sake of the man who told you and for con-

science' sake— [29]the other man's conscience, I mean, not yours. For why should my freedom be judged by another's conscience? [30]If I take part in the meal with thankfulness, why am I denounced because of something I thank God for?

[31]So whether you eat or drink or whatever you do, do it all for the glory of God. [32]Do not cause anyone to stumble, whether Jews, Greeks or the church of God— [33]even as I try to please everybody in every way. For I am not seeking my own good but the good of many, so that they may be saved.

Egypt by the hand of God. First there were ten plagues that decimated Egypt, while the land where the Israelites dwelt was unharmed. In the tenth plague, death spread to every Egyptian family, while all of Israel was spared. The Israelites then fled with gold and silver plundered from the Egyptians. When the Egyptians pursued, God destroyed the enemy beneath the sea, covering every Egyptian chariot while Israel was delivered. After this supernatural salvation, while they waited for Moses, Israel entered into idolatry. The people took gold and silver and fashioned it with their own hands, making shapes from their imaginations. They molded it into a calf and worshiped it as the god who had delivered them out of Egypt!

In this example we can see clearly the meaning of idolatry. The invisible God of heaven and earth, who cannot be made into any shape or form, watched the Israelites fashioning gold and silver into the form of a calf. He responded to Moses in Exodus 32:9–10, "I have seen these people, and they are a stiff-necked people. Now leave me alone, so that my anger may burn against them, and that I may destroy them. Then I will make you into a great nation." Instead of worshiping the living God in spirit and in truth and acknowledging that *we* are created in *God's* image, idolatry attempts to create *god* in an image that is acceptable to *us*. Notice what follows, a sin that is found in almost all the recorded examples of idolatry in the Bible: immorality.

A fundamental question emerges—why did God care? Why did God, who could blot out these people in an instant, care? We have a clue to this in Deuteronomy 7:7–9. He said in that passage, "The LORD did not set his affection on you because you were more numerous than other peoples, for you were the fewest of all peoples. But it was because *the LORD loved you* and kept the oath he swore to your forefathers that he brought you out with a mighty hand and redeemed you from the land of slavery. Know therefore that the LORD your God is God; he is the faithful God, keeping his covenant of love to a thousand generations of those who love him." The answer is this: God hated idolatry in his people because he loved them. He redeemed them to display his love and mercy. Then his people, the recipients of such great redeeming love, turned to idolatry at the first challenge. His love was treated with contempt.

That is why Israel, with her offenses, was called an adulteress. God called Israel his wife, just as the church is called the bride of Christ (2 Cor. 11:2). There is nothing worse that a wife can do to despise the love of a faithful husband than to play the harlot. That is what Israel did repeatedly. Notice these examples. Jeremiah asked, "Where then are the gods you made for yourselves? . . . for you have as many gods as you have towns, O Judah" (Jer. 2:28). He continued in Jeremiah 3:1, "But you have lived as a prostitute with many lovers." Then he said in Jeremiah 3:9, "She defiled the land and committed adultery with stone and wood." Yet here is the message from the Lord, her husband, whose love was so great. " 'Return, faithless people,' declares the LORD, 'for I am your husband. . . . But like a woman unfaithful to her husband, so you have been unfaithful to me, O house of Israel' declares the LORD." Almost all the prophets spoke using the same parallel. They expressed the grief of a true love broken by an unfaithful lover. That is what idolatry is when God's people practice it. It is the adulterous choice of another, upon whom they set their affection. That is what Israel did to the God who redeemed her because of his great love. She despised God, and because he truly loved his bride, he hated her unfaithfulness. In Ezekiel 16:42 he said he would put a stop to Israel's idolatry. "Then my wrath against you will subside and my jealous anger will turn away from you. I will be calm and no longer angry." God hates idolatry because it is a sin against his love.

Pagans feast and practice idolatry, but we Christians feast and commune with Christ. Our feast, the Lord's Supper, is the heart of Christian worship. To understand it, we must go back again to the beginning of Israel's history as a nation. We can understand the Lord's Supper only by understanding the Passover. In the Passover, God's people had communion with him. The elements of the Passover celebration included the lamb and the blood of the lamb. The meal was a reminder that it took the killing of a lamb to redeem them from bondage. The blood, which was spread on the doorposts and side posts of their homes, reminded them of the Destroyer Angel that passed over and spared all who were inside. Those homes were covered by the blood of the lamb. For more than fifteen hundred years, Israel celebrated this feast. They did this to remember their great deliverance from the hands of the Egyptians by the power of God. In this celebration Israel remembered that they enjoyed their freedom as a people only because God loved them. In Deuteronomy 7:8 we read, "It was because the LORD loved you and kept the oath that he swore to your forefathers that he brought you out with a mighty hand and redeemed you from the land of slavery."

On Passover night, the night of his betrayal, Jesus took the bread, which was handed out communally as the *aphikōmen*, the body of the lamb, and said, "This is my body . . . which is broken for you. Do this in remembrance of me." He took the wine, which is the cup of blessing and redemption at the end of the meal, and said, "This is my blood of the new covenant, which is poured out for many for the forgiveness of sins." He changed just one word of the phrase that had originally instituted the Old Covenant. In Exodus 24:8, Moses sprinkled the altar and the people with the blood saying, "This is the blood of the covenant." But in the fullness of times, when Jesus came, it was not the blood of bulls or goats that redeemed, but as he said, "*My* blood of the new covenant."

It was love that marked the redemption of the Old Covenant people, and it is *love unparalleled* that marks our redemption in the New Covenant. We read, "God so loved the world that he gave his one and only Son, that whoever believes in him shall not perish but have eternal life" (John 3:16). In 1 John 4:10 we read, "This is love: not that we loved God, but that he loved us and sent his Son as an atoning sacrifice for our sins." Galatians 2:20 has the most personal expression of his love: he "loved me and gave himself for me." The spiritual remembrance for God's people is no longer our redemption from the bondage of slavery in Egypt, but our redemption from bondage to sin and death, secured by Jesus Christ. Indeed we can say that the glory of God is revealed in his love for helpless, wretched sinners like you and me. The Lord's Supper unites us in fellowship with this loving God, for we are partaking of Christ. In the communion, we are identifying with Christ; we are joining ourselves to Christ.

If we participate in the religious activities of idolaters, we are participating in idolatry. It doesn't matter if we believe that we are not engaging in idolatry in our hearts. It doesn't matter if we feel strong enough or free enough to handle it. We are idolaters, and idolatry will eventually destroy us. We must never, in any way, compromise our relationship to Christ with any attachment or affiliation with an idol. Idols will pull us from Christ, and we, like Israel, will be lured inevitably into spiritual, and possibly physical, adultery. Paul urged us to "flee from idolatry" (1 Cor. 10:14), and this is important because of several realities.

1. *Idolatry is dangerous.* "If you think you are standing firm, be careful that you don't fall!" (1 Cor. 10:12). There is no room for presumption. Idols are nothing in reality, but they ensnare two-thirds of the world and a satanic influence keeps them from Christ. When an individual starts down the road of idolatry, he receives certain pleasures consistent with the practices. The hope of extrication from such evil diminishes dramatically at that point. If such behavior continues, although the people of God warn him and the Word of God is repeatedly brought to bear, the participant of

such practices will suffer, and those around him or her will suffer. Be very humble, then, in this issue of idols. You must avoid idolatry because of its tremendous dangers.

2. *Idolatry is demonic.* This is what 1 Corinthians 10:20 means when it speaks of "participants with demons." It is a participation with the powers of darkness. It is a fellowship with all that hate Jesus Christ. This participation with demons is far more evil, and far more involved, than we might ever think. It is an evil that is vast and for which the church should engage in prayer and fasting. Avoid idolatry because it is demonic.

3. *When we take the Lord's Supper we are communing with Christ.* In essence, going to the Lord's Supper is a renunciation of Satan, just as dining with demons is a renunciation of Christ (1 Cor. 10:20). Our participation in the Lord's Supper is an actual communion with Christ. The word used is *koinonia.* This speaks not of our fellowship with each other, which is how Christians use the word today. This word refers to our fellowship with the risen Christ. We are in the deepest possible relationship with Christ. It is a real participation in the grace purchased by Christ, which he communicates to his people, most especially as it is evidenced in the Lord's Supper. Because our union and communion with Christ is so intense and special, nothing, especially not an idol of any kind, must ever be allowed to enter our lives.

4. *Participation in the Lord's Supper is a participation in the life of Christ.* It is "Christ in us, the hope of glory." It is, "I no longer live, but Christ lives in me" (Gal.

2:20). That is how the relationship is so intimate. In partaking of the Lord's Supper, we are partaking of all that Christ has for us in living, dying, rising, and returning. We are those for whom he died and rose. We are those for whom he will return. Even the slightest attachment to the world and its spiritual system will destroy the power of a Christian participating in the life of Christ.

5. *We cannot commune with Christ and demons.* Paul made this clear in 1 Corinthians 10:16 when he said, "Is not the cup of thanksgiving for which we give thanks a participation in the blood of Christ? And is not the bread that we break a participation in the body of Christ?" Compare this with 1 Corinthians 10:20–21, "No, but the sacrifices of pagans are offered to demons, not to God, and I do not want you to be participants with demons. You cannot drink the cup of the Lord and the cup of demons too; you cannot have a part in both the Lord's table and the table of demons." The Lord's Supper is a means of grace commemorating the finished work of Christ, while idolatry is a celebration in the world of demons. "The sacrifices of pagans are offered to demons and not to God." There is no common ground. You are either in union with Christ, or you are in union with demons, because the Lord's Supper shows the reality of the two worlds in collision.

Paul is dogmatic that the people of God shouldn't be participants with demons. He took this strong stand while the church was readily and casually entertaining idolatry. Likewise, one of the big problems in our culture is that people try to live in both worlds at the same time. Living in this way means that they are not living with Christ. There is no one who can be in fellowship with Christ while having fellowship in the demonic realm. Communion is participation in the body and blood of Christ. You must flee idolatry because it is antithetical to everything Christian.

6. *The Lord's Supper gives us grace to love Christ and resist idolatry.* The Lord's Supper is a means of grace. In other words, when we partake in faith, we receive grace from the Lord. He gives us comfort by his presence, assurance that he has forgiven our sins, and strength to continue striving for the faith. That is why we should celebrate the Lord's Supper frequently, that we might benefit from such graces from God. It is also why we should flee idolatry and anything that would keep us from enjoying these benefits. We, as God's people, must not have anything to do with idolatry, including the lusts of the flesh, because we are consecrated to Christ and live in unbroken fellowship with him.

7. *We are in relationship with one another.* As Paul said, "We, who are many, are one body" (1 Cor. 10:17). The same bond that unites us to our head, Jesus, also unites us to one another. By involving ourselves in idolatry, we rupture our relationship to Christ. But we rupture as well our relationship to each other. We must flee idolatry because our union with Christ also brings us into relationship with one another.

8. *We must avoid idolatry by fleeing from it.* The word *flee* is in a present continuous tense. This indicates that we

are to run from idolatry continually. The idols of this world will surely lure us, steadily and persistently. We may not even realize what is happening until we are deeply in their clutches. We must understand that idolatry is not just objects of wood and stone but is all that we set our hearts on. If we do not flee when it is easy, what makes us think that we can flee when it is difficult? If you are aware of the dangers of something idolatrous to your heart, keep your distance from it.

This passage concludes by asking the question, "Do you know what you are doing?" Do you realize that by allowing yourself to be seduced by the idols of this age and the idols of your hearts, you are provoking the Lord to jealousy? Jealousy is something terrible indeed. As we read in Deuteronomy 32:21, "They have made me jealous by what is no god and angered me with their worthless idols." How can we who belong to Christ, who have been redeemed by the blood of Christ, allow ourselves to be wed to any but Christ? A husband's jealousy and wrath would flare up if his wife said that he was not her only love interest, but other men were as well. His anger would be completely justified in such a situation. Here the apostle reminds the church that if we divide our love between Christ and idols, we will kindle his passionate anger, because he is our husband. To him our total allegiance and affection are due, for he has loved us unto death, even the death on the cross. We must remain chaste Christians. The first way is to "flee from all idolatry."

## HEADSHIP IN THE CHURCH

I n Galatians 5:1, Paul wrote, "It is for freedom that Christ has set us free. Stand firm, then, and do not let yourselves be burdened again by a yoke of slavery." I believe that the teaching in 1 Corinthians 11 contributes to the freedom referred to here. It does this because it is concerned to teach a proper view of worship. It is a passage that speaks to men and women. This section of Scripture began and ended the same way, with an appeal to apostolic teaching. The apostle began by praising this church for remembering him in everything and for holding to the teachings just as they were passed on to them (1 Cor. 11:2). He ended by saying, "We have no other practice—nor do the churches of God" (1 Cor. 11:16). These issues are to be decided by nothing less than the teaching of the apostles in the Word of God.

Nothing is more precious to us than our freedom to worship God. We must understand the basis of our worship, as well as how it is to be expressed. In worship, men and women stand before the throne of God, praising his glorious name in

### 1 CORINTHIANS 11:2-16

²I praise you for remembering me in everything and for holding to the teachings, just as I passed them on to you.

³Now I want you to realize that the head of every man is Christ, and the head of the woman is man, and the head of Christ is God. ⁴Every man who prays or prophesies with his head covered dishonors his head. ⁵And every woman who prays or prophesies with her head uncovered dishonors her head—it is just as though her head were shaved. ⁶If a woman does not cover her head, she should have her hair cut off; and if it is a disgrace for a woman to have her hair cut or shaved off, she should cover her head. ⁷A man ought not to cover his head, since he is the image and glory of God; but the woman is the glory of man. ⁸For man did not come from

prayer and prophecy, by word and song. The apostle wants us to realize how it is that we may come into the presence of God and speak at all! He does this by teaching us about our relationship to God and to one another.

Because worship is so important, the worship of God is the target of Satan's most vicious assaults. He wants the praises of God to be silenced on the earth! He wants the voices of men and women glorifying God to be stopped. It is interesting to note that the two worship activities mentioned in this passage—prayer and prophecy—are the two offensive weapons we are given to wage war against "principalities and powers . . . against the spiritual forces of wickedness in the heavenly realms." In the public worship of God, we not only stand before the face of God. We stand woman, but woman from man; [9]neither was man created for woman, but woman for man. [10]For this reason, and because of the angels, the woman ought to have a sign of authority on her head.

[11]In the Lord, however, woman is not independent of man, nor is man independent of woman. [12]For as woman came from man, so also man is born of woman. But everything comes from God. [13]Judge for yourselves: Is it proper for a woman to pray to God with her head uncovered? [14]Does not the very nature of things teach you that if a man has long hair, it is a disgrace to him, [15]but that if a woman has long hair, it is her glory? For long hair is given to her as a covering. [16]If anyone wants to be contentious about this, we have no other practice—nor do the churches of God.

up and face the forces of hell as well, with prayer and the prophetic word. It is essential that in this warfare we are clear about how we stand before God. Thus the apostle wrote as the foundational words of his instructions, "I want you to realize that the head of every man is Christ, and that the head of the woman is man, and that the head of Christ is God" (1 Cor. 11:3).

We must look at the subject of headship. This statement opens in 1 Corinthians 11 by saying that Christ is the head of every man. Is the author James Bordwine correct when he writes, "We understand 'man' to mean males in general"?[1] I

1. James Bordwine, *The Pauline Doctrine of Male Headship* (Vancouver: Wash.: Westminster Institute, 1996), 24.

believe rather that Charles Hodge is correct when he wrote, "The meaning is every believer because it is the relationship of Christ to the church and not Christ's relationship to the human family that is characteristically expressed by this term."[2] Hodge is supported by Ephesians 1:22–23, "God placed all things under his feet and appointed him to be head over everything for the church, which is his body, the fullness of him who fills everything in every way." Christ is the head of all believers, not only males.

The next part of 1 Corinthians 11:3 says that the head of the wife is her husband. Whenever the words *gunē* and *anēr* are used, they are understood based on their context. They can be translated as "wife and husband" or "woman and man." For an example of how important it is to translate these words accurately in context, notice in Ephesians 5:25 that it does not say, "Men, love women," although exactly the same words are used here as in 1 Corinthians 11:3. Of course not! It is, "Husbands, love your wives." We can see this in several other references as well: Ephesians 5:22, 24, 28; Colossians 3:18–19; and 1 Timothy 3:12. First Peter 3:1 says, "Wives . . . be submissive to your husbands," not "Women, be submissive to men." In 1 Peter 3:7 the apostle said, "Husbands . . . be considerate as you live with your wives." These passages teach that it is the husband who is the head of his wife, not men who are the head of women in general. If, as some suggest, men are the heads of all women, then what would a husband's headship mean? It would mean that a man's wife was to be in submission to every Tom, Dick, and Harry, which would be absurd.

---

2. Charles Hodge, *A Commentary on 1 and 2 Corinthians* (Edinburgh: Banner of Truth Trust, 1857), 207.

It is important to translate this sentence accurately here, because the context is that of the husband and wife, not men and women in general.

Finally, we read, "the head of Christ is God." Christ in his earthly ministry was under authority. He said, "I have come in my Father's name" (John 5:43). Again he said, "I do nothing on my own but speak just what the Father taught me" (John 8:28); "I have not come on my own, but he sent me" (v. 42); "I honor my Father" (v. 49); "I am not seeking glory for myself" (v. 50); and "My Father . . . is the one who glorifies me" (v. 54). Jesus understood that he *had* authority because he was *under* authority. As he said, "I did not speak of my own accord, but the Father who sent me commanded me what to say and how to say it" (John 12:49).

Even though the head of Christ is God, it is clear in the Scriptures that the Son is equal to God. In fact, the Pharisees tried to kill him based on the accusation, "He was . . . making himself equal with God" (John 5:18). John quoted Christ, "I and the Father are one" (John 10:30), using the same word for oneness that characterizes the relationship of the husband and wife in Genesis 2:24. It says there of the husband and wife, "The two shall become one." The headship in all three cases is a headship within an intimate union of love: the love between God the Father and God the Son, the love between Christ and the church, and the love between a husband and a wife. Reviewing the relationship of the husband and wife, as it is patterned after the relationship of God the Father and Christ, we are reminded that Christ *had* authority because he was *under* authority. Likewise we see in 1 Corinthians 11:3–16 that the woman *has* authority because she is *under* authority. She is not only under the authority of God who is the head of Christ, and the authority of Christ who is the head of every man, but she has an additional authority to whom she may appeal. She has the authority to pray and prophesy because she is under the authority of her husband, who is her head.

In this passage the apostle applied the doctrine of headship to the practice of the public worship of God. What concerned him in this section was how God's people may pray and prophesy—not whether they may pray and prophesy. Men and women were told in what manner they were to come and speak before the Lord in the great assembly. Remember, this passage was not dealing with elders and the rule of the church. It was not speaking about pastoral prayer or preaching from the pulpit. Nor was it talking about the leadership of the church. This passage was speaking about the members of the congregation. It is clear from 1 Corinthians 11:5 that when the elders open the worship service for a time of congregational prayer, men and women may come before the Lord in prayer—not just in their hearts but with their lips. The apostle was not speaking here about women involved in private prayer but about the prayer life of the congregation in worship. The call to open the worship with a time of psalms, testimonies, and encouragement, is for men and women who may speak. The text in 1 Corinthians 14 says, "Everyone has a psalm, or a word of exhortation," and the apostle was reminding the worshipers by what authority everyone can pray or prophesy in the worship of God—by the authority of the head of the church, Jesus Christ. While all people have Christ as their head, the woman has an additional head, her husband.

A husband, in exercising headship, does not need to focus on his authority. He needs to focus on being a merciful and loving husband. I do not know of any woman who has entered into marriage so that she would be ruled by a man, but so that she would be loved. This, my friends, is what marriage is all about. While it may seem easy, it is probably the most difficult lesson all men, including Christian men, have to learn.

Let me at this point briefly raise an issue where the apostle seemed to be inconsistent. In 1 Corinthians 14:34 he commanded women to be silent. Was Paul contradicting himself? Since we know this cannot be the case, we have to ask what he meant. Was he calling for absolute silence from women? Almost none would say that a woman can't sing, so it can't be absolute silence. Since she can pray or prophesy, the question then is, what is the silence he has in mind?

I believe this passage teaches that there are times when the woman is to be silent. The times that are in view are those times during the preaching of the Word of God that are undertaken by the pastor or elders of the church. That is when the prophetic Word of God is exposited to the congregation. Perhaps this is all he has in mind. Certainly some argue that way. But I think the context argues for a silence that goes beyond the preaching of the Word of God. The passage is talking about confusion and discord in the church because people were speaking in foreign languages without interpretation. Several people at once were bringing revelations. Others were bringing prophecies, often without interpretation. In the immediate context here, the apostle said that the "spirits of the prophets [which obviously included women], are subject to the control of the prophets. For God is not a God of disorder but of peace" (1 Cor. 14:33). It is in the next words that Paul called for silence from the women. The women were not to add to the confusion by interrupting or questioning or interpreting but rather were to maintain self-control by keeping silent at these times. They were to deal with their concerns about the prophetic teaching ministry, which is different than the prophetic ministry, quietly at home with their husbands.

R. C. Sproul says in his article on 1 Corinthians 14, which he entitles "Women Be Silent," that if a woman has a gift of prophecy, which he grants does occur, that she must use it privately. He doesn't deny that she may have this gift but only that she must never use it publicly in the worship service. Is she then, as Sproul suggests, to reveal God's truth and proclaim God's Word inside of her closet? Is this why God poured out his Spirit on all people, so that women could prophesy where none could hear them?

What I am suggesting is very different from a recent Reformed volume that says, "Terms like male dominance, subjection, subjugation, rightly express what the Bible teaches. Society's like or dislike of them is of no consequence. These words need to be utilized more frequently and with greater conviction."[3] These men would teach a doctrine of male subjugation of every woman with greater and greater conviction. Listen to how the dictionary defines subjugation: "To conquer, to make subservient in any way, to enslave." That is what these men are calling for in marriage—the enslavement of women, with "greater frequency and greater conviction." Why should any woman marry if this is what marriage is meant to be? Why should she willingly see her life enslaved?

These men do not recognize that their teaching is as big a

3. Bordwine, *The Pauline Doctrine of Male Headship*, 135.

problem as the feminist teaching they so detest. In fact, when you realize that men have done this, that is, subjugated women for thousands of years, you can only wonder how it took so long for the feminist movement to form. It is unfortunately rare to find a marriage in which the husband recognizes that he bears the responsibility of headship and exercises it in humility and love rather than in force and authoritarianism. While I too am against so much of what the feminist movement advocates, I understand why it has emerged. I believe that if Christian men had been the servant leaders in the home, rather than conceited chauvinists, the feminist movement would have died a quick and easy death. If men had sought ways to see the gifts and talents of their wives developed and utilized rather than taking a beautiful person and making her into little more than a personal slave, if men had not twisted this doctrine of headship, we would not have the current problems between men and women in our society.

I am tired of hearing that feminists are responsible for the breakdown of the family. We need to put the responsibility where it belongs—on the heads of homes. They have not been the loving heads that they were called to be by Christ, but rather, petty tyrants. For over twenty-five years, I have seen in marriage counseling that much of their behavior is an insult to the Savior whose life and sacrifice is to be the pattern for their headship in the home. The doctrinal foundation of 1 Corinthians 11 calls for husbands to be men like Christ. It calls for the church to be a place where men and women together praise and glorify God. As John Piper and Wayne Grudem's book, *Recovering Biblical Manhood and Womanhood: A Response to Evangelical Feminism,* so aptly puts it, "We should affirm the participation of women in prayer and prophecy in the church. Their contribution should not be slighted or ignored."[4]

The following is a summary of the apostle's teaching on headship in the life of the family and of the church.

1. *A biblical view of marriage.* " 'In that day,' declares the LORD, 'you will call me "my husband"; you will no longer call me "my master." I will remove the names of the Baals from her lips; no longer will their names be invoked. . . . I will betroth you to me forever. I will betroth you in righteousness and justice, in love and compassion. I will betroth you in faithfulness, and you will acknowledge the LORD' " (Hos. 2:16–17, 19–20). This is the view of marriage that God's men need to possess not a ruler/subject relationship but a relationship forged in righteousness and justice, love and compassion.

2. *A biblical view of headship and submission.* Piper writes, "Biblical headship for the husband is the divine calling to take primary responsibility for Christlike leadership, protection, and provision . . . submission refers to a wife's divine calling to honor and affirm her husband's leadership and helps carry it through according to her gifts."[5] This is one of the reasons why it is so important for men to encourage and facilitate the gifts of their wives: together they use these gifts to advance the kingdom of God. Headship and submission are the tools by which the husband and wife express their

---

4. John Piper and Wayne Grudem, *Recovering Biblical Manhood and Womanhood,* (Wheaton, Ill.: Crossway, 1991), 139.
5. Ibid., 61.

ministry as partners in the church. Because of this, it is time for men to realize that the cooking of food and the cleaning of the home is not what God meant in calling the wife a "helper." A servant can cook, a maid can clean, but the wife is called to be a special helper on their road together to Zion. I am not saying that this doesn't involve household responsibilities, but household responsibilities are not absent from a husband either.

3. *A biblical view of interdependence.* The apostle has laid out the organizing principle of a husband's headship as a reflection of the headship in the Godhead. What follows is the implied teaching here (although specific in other passages) of a woman's submission to her husband. In 1 Corinthians 11:11 there is a qualification to the above principle, which helps to reinforce what headship and submission are meant to be. That qualification is the mutual interdependence of a husband and his wife. The apostle said, "In the Lord, however, woman is not independent of man, nor is man independent of woman." It is not all men and all women who are interdependent, but a husband and a wife. This verse is important because it is the biblical repudiation of any sense of inferiority of either gender in relationship to the other. In the next verse, Paul continued, "For as woman came from man, so also is man born of woman." The conclusion of his argument is telling, "Everything comes from God." Our equality does not preclude different roles. Only men can become fathers, and only women can become mothers, and nothing can ever, or should ever, change that.

Men will never bear children or nurse babies. Women will never be the elders in the church. There is interdependence, while at the same time there is well-defined role differentiation.

4. *A biblical view of interdependence and ministry in the church.* This interdependence of the husband and his wife extend to the realm of ministry. An elder is to be "the husband of one wife," meaning a man who is devoted to his wife and an excellent manager of his home. He works alongside a wife who is also, according to Proverbs 31, an excellent manager of her home. A man whose life is like this is considered suitable for the eldership, because when he is an elder, he will be working side by side with his wife. This thought is alluded to in the requirements for the elder when it presents requirements for his wife as well as the wives of deacons. It says, "Their wives are to be women worthy of respect, not malicious talkers but temperate and trustworthy in everything" (1 Tim. 3:11). Why? Because they will be working together. They are partners in life, and that partnership extends to the ministry. Calvin said regarding this text in Timothy, "Likewise the wives . . . means the wives of both the deacons and elders . . . for they must be aids to their husbands in office, which cannot be unless their behavior excel that of others." It is truly amazing that this partnership that God instituted from the beginning has been so neglected by the church.

Although many Bible teachers assert that the issues of 1 Corinthians 11 are not vital to the life of the church, these are issues at the heart of the nature of men and women: headship, church worship and practice, leadership in the church, and marriage and the home. There is quite possibly no other passage of Scripture that is filled with greater practical importance. There is so much at stake, because only when we as men and women understand who we are in Christ will we see the blessing and happiness that God intends for our well-being in the home, in the church, and even in society.

I
f I asked you, "What is the most controversial subject in the Christian church today?" spiritual gifts would quite possibly head the list. Baptists and Presbyterians coexist happily in the same congregation, and premillenialists, amillenialists, and postmillenialists are in the same congregation. Psalm-singing and hymn-singing believers worship in the same congregation. But I have never seen a congregation peacefully embrace one another when the members have divergent views on the gifts. Therefore it is critical to understand this issue biblically. The apostle expressed concern, "Now about spiritual gifts, brothers, I do not want you to be ignorant." In the Christian faith, which is based on truth, ignorance leads to great harm. Tremendous dangers abound if we are ignorant in this area.

There are many controversies on this topic that lead to error. For example, there are those who say that certain gifts continue to exist while others say that not all the gifts still exist in the church today. Another controversy concerns speaking in

> ### 1 CORINTHIANS 12:1-11
>
> [1]Now about spiritual gifts, brothers, I do not want you to be ignorant. [2]You know that when you were pagans, somehow or other you were influenced and led astray to mute idols. [3]Therefore I tell you that no one who is speaking by the Spirit of God says, "Jesus be cursed," and no one can say, "Jesus is Lord," except by the Holy Spirit.
>
> [4]There are different kinds of gifts, but the same Spirit. [5]There are different kinds of service, but the same Lord. [6]There are different kinds of working, but the same God works all of them in all men.

tongues. Yet another involves prophecy or extrabiblical revelation. These questions are only the outworking of far more complicated issues. What does the Bible mean by the term "spiritual gifts"? Do these gifts still exist? Should we try to attain these gifts? What about churches and people who don't have these gifts? Do people still have miraculous gifts? If some gifts no longer manifest themselves, what happened to them? We must ask God for discernment in this area of spiritual gifts, so that we will not be ignorant. We must seek from the Scriptures a resolution to this confusing and controversial subject.

The logical starting point is to begin with the history of this problem in the Corinthian church. We are looking at a church that had many problems and divisions. There is no way for us to understand the problems connected with spiritual gifts without looking at the Corinthian church. In this battle, the apostle took on what was his most difficult task at

> $^7$Now to each one the manifestation of the Spirit is given for the common good. $^8$To one there is given through the Spirit the message of wisdom, to another the message of knowledge by means of the same Spirit, $^9$to another faith by the same Spirit, to another gifts of healing by that one Spirit, $^{10}$to another miraculous powers, to another prophecy, to another distinguishing between spirits, to another speaking in different kinds of tongues, and to still another the interpretation of tongues. $^{11}$All these are the work of one and the same Spirit, and he gives them to each one, just as he determines.

that church up to that time. Previously he had dealt with matters that had a clear direction to resolution. Even though they were terrible situations, the truth about them from the Word of God was easily discernible, whether it was the issue of divisions in the church, lawsuits among brethren, fornication, incest, or homosexuality. But now he needed to bring discipline to all kinds of unruly behavior. What made this difficult was that these practices were already part of the life of the church. The question of whether these manifestations would exist in the church until the end of time had never before been raised.

Just as the church at that time was infused with a kind of unruly ecstasy, so also today, there is a deepened commitment to ecstasy as the standard of truly spiritual behavior. The problem is so bad today in some circles that if you grunt like a pig or roar like a lion in a worship service, you are considered the most spiritual. People from all over the world journey to be part of such an experience. All of this originated with the early mystery religions of Babylon, which had the overarching religious principle of communing with God through ecstatic experiences. Whenever this behavior has been part of the Christian church over the last two thousand years, it has seemed on the surface to be the more spiritual route. It then leaves other forms of Christianity behind as dead. But at the same time, it always leaves in its wake a trail of burned-out, confused, disorganized, and disheartened Christians.

This background brings into focus the concern that Paul had. He said in 1 Corinthians 12:2, "You know that when you were pagans, . . . you were . . . led astray to mute idols." He reminded them about their life as pagans because their present behavior was similar to what it had been before. He was concerned that this behavior signaled a return to paganism. Their interest in this kind of ecstasy was no different from the idolatry they had embraced before their conversions. That is why he reminded them of two things: their former days as pagans and the behavior in which they engaged during those early days. They had been carried away, and that was idolatrous. The word for "carried away" signifies force and power. They weren't given over tamely or meekly but with force and power. They were immersed in worship practices that had nothing to do with worship in the Spirit and truth. The apostle was concerned that the Corinthians would once again embrace false teaching, that they would again be led astray by a form of idolatry that was sweeping the church, a wild ecstasy, and that they would use the gifts of the Spirit in counterfeit ways. He needed to resolve this issue. He needed a solution that could reach the Corinthians who were becoming more and more enmeshed in what was nothing more than a type of idolatry.

One reality supersedes everything else, and it was demonstrated in his solution. He said, "No one who is speaking by the Spirit of God says, 'Jesus be cursed,' and no one can say, 'Jesus is Lord,' except by the Holy Spirit." His opening argument brought the church to the most fundamental question, What do these purported prophets and miracle workers say of Christ? Do they worship or blaspheme Christ? If they openly and sincerely recognize that Jesus Christ is Lord, then they must be acknowledged to be under the influence of the Holy Spirit. If not, then regardless of what they do, that is, regardless of the power or charisma they demonstrate, they must not be treated as true followers of Christ or leaders of Christ's people.

Here, the apostle again offered the first part of his solution. The idol has no voice. It is dumb. It supposedly represents a deity but cannot speak, so there is no voice to which you must listen. A voice that does speak of God must speak with content. That speech must not be nonsensical, incoherent, or illogical. It must point to Christ and focus on Christ. It is to be Christ-centered. It is to be Christ-honoring. It is to be Christ-glorifying. This reveals the purpose of the apostle in addressing this problem, as we see in 1 Corinthians 12:4–7. He did not destroy the idea of gifts in the church. Not at all! Rather, he destroyed the idea of a church so immersed in sensation, so committed to the subjective, so determined to live by its feelings, that the true gifts of the Holy Spirit are not displayed and used but a false and superficial caricature of them. This is, in effect, no different from the mystery religions that are dependent upon subjective sensation rather than the Word of God. What is so terrible about this is that the church is to be a place where the Word is preached and obeyed as the only standard for faith and life.

The apostle's view of the gifts was stated with perfect clarity in 1 Corinthians 12:7, where he said, "Now to each one the manifestation of the Spirit is given for the common good." The gifts have a purpose. They are given for the edification of the church, not for private pleasure or for a demonstration of the supposed highest level of spirituality. They are not a tool to manipulate your inner states or a device to make you feel better. They facilitate the edification of the church. This is the key point. Everything that is given to the church is given for its edification. If it doesn't edify, no matter how exciting it seems, no matter how spiritual it feels—it is not fulfilling the requirements for a spiritual gift.

The apostle Paul said, "Don't be ignorant, but instead you must use your gifts according to knowledge." The church needs knowledge. We live at a time when knowledge is often ridiculed in religion. Even much of supposedly hard science is mysticism and irrationalism. Within Christian circles, what we do many times is simply the outworking of feelings. It is sentimental, subjective, and sweet. This was not the direction of the apostle! He wanted the church to be committed to knowledge—a knowledge that is gained from the Word of God. In part, it is ignorance that is harming the church. Some Christians cannot discern between true and false gifts. Others in the church put the emphasis on the gifts, where it absolutely doesn't belong. I cannot begin to recount the number of times someone has told me that I must "admit that such and such came from God." The fact is, I don't have to agree to anything of the kind! Or people say that I "can't deny" their experience. Of course I wouldn't deny another person's experience. I would argue about the interpretation of that experience!

In spite of these concerns, there is a place for spiritual gifts. They are given to the body of Christ. They belong to the body of Christ. They are for ministry to the body of Christ. It is in this context that I would urge each individual to determine what gifts you have. I would also urge you to use them. The Bible teaches that all have gifts, and all must use their gifts. Only then will the church be built up. Don't wait for others to use their gifts. Use your gifts, and use them now!

There is a diversity of gifts. The Lord has given all different kinds of gifts to the church, so that it will be edified, sanctified, and conformed to Jesus Christ. When these gifts are used with gladness and humility for the common good, they bring Jesus Christ to the world. They are not for pride or for public show. They are for enlarging of the kingdom. If you have a certain gift, it is a gift that has not been given to you for any selfish purpose. You are to use it. If you don't, you will lose it. Maybe our slogan for the church can be "Use it or lose it!" God's people should use their gifts in ministries in various capacities all their lives. Those older people, men and women, who are skilled in particular areas should be advisors to the young.

Like the Corinthians, we too once worshiped dumb idols. Perhaps in Corinth the idols were more tangible—but they were not more real. Even today, there is not a person who has not been enticed by some form of idolatry. The warning to the church is still relevant. In Corinth, they turned the gifts into idols. They hurled themselves after the sensationalism that had earlier characterized their idolatrous lives. Now again, we are warned to make sure that we are not idolatrously attached to gifts rather than Christ. There are those who say that you are not a real Christian if you don't have certain gifts—that without these gifts you are nothing more than a dead Christian. They say that the mark of a truly Spirit-filled Christian is to have a certain gift that to the apostle wasn't even that special, while to some contemporary churches it is a sign of real spirituality.

Let's look at the highest gift of the Spirit, the ability to savingly acknowledge that Jesus Christ is Lord. Only through a personal relationship with Jesus Christ can we ever have the love of God to manifest to others. Let us not forget that the loftiest position in the universe is to be in the family of God. This comes from a true acknowledgment of Christ, and there is nothing that is greater. If you know Christ, you have, as Peter says, all that is necessary for blessedness forever.

Every believer is encouraged to be knowledgeable about the gifts, to study the word of God about the gifts, and to seek after all that God would have you seek after. Most especially, you are encouraged to use your gifts for the upbuilding and edifying of the church. In the process, remember the most important thing. There is nothing greater than to know Christ. There is nothing more blessed than to be in relationship to Christ. No matter how great your gift, if your heart is hardened toward God, you will not be blessed and the church will not be edified. When you know and love Christ, you will use your gifts to bless his children and build up the church.

The apostle didn't want us to be ignorant about spiritual gifts. Yet there is great ignorance and foolishness concerning spiritual gifts in the church today. Our predecessor, the Corinthian church, was filled with problems concerning the correct use of the gifts. They had immersed themselves in ecstatic experiences and lost sight of the proper place and use of the gifts in the life of the church.

The gifts of the Spirit are best understood when we know the person and work of the Holy Spirit. He is God (2 Cor. 13:14). He is the third person of the Trinity. He is the Comforter, the one who comes alongside us, to help and encourage. We read in John 14:26 that the Holy Spirit will "teach you all things and will remind you of everything I have said to you." In John 15:26, he "goes out from the Father" and "will testify about me [Jesus]"; in John 16:14, he "will bring glory to me [Jesus]"; in Romans 8:16, he testifies that "we are God's children"; and in Romans 8:26, the Holy Spirit "intercedes for us."

The church is baptized by the Holy Spirit. This is the en-

## 1 CORINTHIANS 12:1–11

¹Now about spiritual gifts, brothers, I do not want you to be ignorant. ²You know that when you were pagans, somehow or other you were influenced and led astray to mute idols. ³Therefore I tell you that no one who is speaking by the Spirit of God says, "Jesus be cursed," and no one can say, "Jesus is Lord," except by the Holy Spirit.

⁴There are different kinds of gifts, but the same Spirit. ⁵There are different kinds of service, but the same Lord. ⁶There are different kinds of working, but the same God works all of them in all men.

tire body of Christ, not some select individuals. In Acts 2, the Holy Spirit came upon all the believers, not just a select few. He gives power, as we read in Luke 24:49, "You will be clothed with power from on high." In Acts 1:8 we see the purpose of such a power baptism, "You will receive power when the Holy Spirit comes on you, and *you will be my witnesses.*" The purpose of the baptism of the Holy Spirit is for the church to be a witness throughout the world. We read in Ephesians 4:8 that when Christ ascended, he "gave gifts to men," gifts which testified to the authenticity of the gospel. Hebrews 2:4 teaches that this great salvation was confirmed to us by "signs, wonders and various miracles and gifts of the Holy Spirit distributed according to his will." These gifts were given, Paul said in 1 Corinthians 12:7, "for the common good"; in 1 Corinthians 14:5, 12 for the edification of the church; in Ephesians 4:12 so that the church body would be equipped for the work of

<sup>7</sup>Now to each one the manifestation of the Spirit is given for the common good. <sup>8</sup>To one there is given through the Spirit the message of wisdom, to another the message of knowledge by means of the same Spirit, <sup>9</sup>to another faith by the same Spirit, to another gifts of healing by that one Spirit, <sup>10</sup>to another miraculous powers, to another prophecy, to another distinguishing between spirits, to another speaking in different kinds of tongues, and to still another the interpretation of tongues. <sup>11</sup>All these are the work of one and the same Spirit, and he gives them to each one, just as he determines.

ministry; and in 1 Peter 4:10 so that we would serve others and faithfully administer God's grace.

When we are converted, we receive the Holy Spirit. We are baptized by the Holy Spirit. We receive power for ministry from the Holy Spirit. We are filled with the Holy Spirit. In fact, without the Holy Spirit, we cannot be true Christians and cannot do anything that is consistent with the Christian life. We need the Holy Spirit, and he gives his gifts liberally to the church so that it will accomplish his purposes of revealing and glorifying Christ to the world, as well as serving and ministering to each other.

To know what the spiritual gifts are, we must go to the Word of God. We must be careful not to confuse them with natural abilities that we and non-Christians might have. Understanding the gifts in this way does not demean the full range of natural gifts God's people might possess. Since we are called to seek spiritual gifts, this is not something we naturally possess in our assemblies but rather something that we must earnestly, honestly, and deliberately seek.

Spiritual gifts come from God. We may find ourselves at times surprised with the gifts we have. While they may be consistent with our natural abilities, they might be quite divergent. For example, when someone tells me that they want to leave the church because they can't use their spiritual gift of music, as someone who played the organ once told me (we don't use an organ in our congregation), I respond that this is not a spiritual gift. It is a talent that any person can possess and is not the same as a Spirit-directed and Spirit-supervised gift that may make use of our talents but is not to be identified with those talents. If people are not identifying and utilizing their gifts for the body of Christ, then the body cannot possibly function as God intended.

## WISDOM

These gifts from the Holy Spirit are crucial to the proper growth of the body of Christ. First are words of wisdom. Could the author be right, who says that this gift both supernaturally reveals the mind of God as well as his specific purposes for all kinds of specifics of individual people, places and things? Is he correct in his understanding that this gift opens the receiver of it to the audible voice of God and visits by angels? Should the gift of words of wisdom be understood in this fashion? *Logos,* or "word," refers to speech. *Sophia,* or "wisdom," refers to the ability to apply God's Word and God's will. This gift has to do with the mind—a mind that is given over to God, and not just in a personal sense. It is making known

God's will, from God's Word, the purpose and plan for the church. To have a word of wisdom means to be able to present the deep spiritual realities that affect and undergird the lives of God's people, especially as they apply in the situation of the church or of individuals at a particular time. A good biblical counselor possesses this gift. In 1 Chronicles 12:32 we see this gift in the children of Issachar, of whom it is written, the "men of Isachar . . . understood the times and knew what Israel had to do." It is a gift of spiritual discernment, and when it is applied to the lives of God's people, it helps them to live in a way that fulfills the will of God.

## KNOWLEDGE

The second gift is similar, the word of knowledge. The word *knowledge* is used in the New Testament more than three hundred times, with incredible variation of meaning. Along these lines, is it correct to think of this gift, as a supernatural revelation of actual facts in the mind of God, even going so far as to reveal the exact location of some event, as is the idea of yet another author? That would not be the meaning of the gift in the passage here. God spoke to the writers of the Scriptures, such as the apostle Paul, and now we no longer need to be spoken to directly by God. We can refer to those Scriptures.

This gift refers to a word of knowledge in the broadest sense. Since the gift of wisdom is the ability to *apply* the Word of God, the gift of knowledge is the Spirit-given ability to *understand* the Word of God. It is a gift of knowing in a deep and powerful way what the Word of God teaches. That is what knowledge is all about! Knowledge refers to profound insight into the Word of God. Why make this gift into supernatural revelations, when knowledge is always connected with the Word of God, and particularly the ability to really understand the Word? It is a gift from God, and like all the gifts, it is supernaturally derived, but it is not to be understood in the more limited sense of a direct audible communication of knowledge. That is not necessary in our age because the Word of God is here! Since knowledge indicates content, utilizing this gift requires research and investigation as we strive to correctly understand the teachings of the apostles and prophets.

Third, there is the gift of faith. Since this is a gift given only to some Christians, it cannot refer to saving faith that every believer possesses. It seems that this gift is a higher measure of what every believer possesses. Apparently some believers have the ability to trust God beyond the ability that is given to others. They can, for example, trust God in the most difficult situations, when circumstances seem utterly impossible. A person with such faith is likely to find expression of this in prayer, where he might cry out, "Father, I know you always hear me," as Jesus prayed. This is the person who really believes that mountains of impossibility can be moved by faith, and he doesn't let the impracticalities stop him from interceding with God.

### HEALING

In the fourth place, there is the gift of healings, which is mentioned three times in this twelfth chapter of 1 Corinthians. In all three passages in the Greek, the word *healing* is in the plural. Perhaps this is because of the wide diversity of illnesses and afflictions that received healing. This gift includes crushing the devil, because Acts 10:38 tells us that Jesus healed "all who were under the power of the devil." It involves authenticating the Word, as we find in Acts 4:29–30, "Enable your servants to speak your word with great boldness. Stretch out your hand to heal." It substantiates the resurrection of Jesus, in Acts 3:15–16, "You killed the author of life, but God raised him from the dead. . . . By faith in the name of Jesus, this man whom you see and know was made strong. It is Jesus' name and the faith that comes through him that has given this complete healing to him, as you can all see." It turns people to God, as we read in Acts 9:32–35 where Peter said to a man, "Jesus Christ heals you." Everyone who lived in that area "turned to the Lord." Healings were a means to bring glory to God. In Luke 13:17 Jesus healed a woman, and immediately she began to glorify God. In Matthew 9:6, when Jesus healed a paralyzed man, we read that the people "were filled with awe; and they praised God."

## Miracles

Fifth, there is the gift of miracles. As with faith, miracles are mentioned three times in this chapter (1 Cor. 12:10, 28–29). Three words are used for miracle, the first being *dynamis,* which means "power." It is a word that depicts a miracle as a manifestation of divine power. The second word is *sēmeion,* which means "sign" and describes a miracle as that which authenticates the mission of the doer. Third, there is *teras,* which is "a wonder." All three words are used in Hebrews 2:4, where the passage teaches that God bears witness to his great salvation with "signs, wonders and various miracles." A miracle is an intervention in nature. It is a temporary cessation of the laws that govern our world (as we commonly understand them as laws). Some of the biblical miracles include creation, the deliverance of Israel out of Egypt, the sun standing still when Joshua battled the Amorites, the virgin birth of Christ, the raising of Lazarus, and the raising of believers to eternal life with resurrection bodies on the last day.

I mention these examples because in each we see the cessation of natural law. Many believers speak all too casually about miracles. They say, "The man called me about that job right after I prayed. It's a miracle." But it is not a miracle, as wonderful as it may be. Or we hear, "I was in a terrible accident—the car rolled over five times, and I wasn't hurt. It's a miracle." Again, this isn't a miracle, though God's care over us is great. The people in the New Testament were often astounded by Jesus' miracles. Even Herod, in Luke 23:8, was glad when he finally met Jesus, because "he hoped to see him perform some miracle." True miracles always attract interest, but they don't sustain that interest. In John 6, Jesus fed five thousand people, and large crowds gathered around him. But when he preached the Word of life to the people, we read that they "began to argue sharply among themselves," and "from this time many of his disciples turned back and no longer followed him" (John 6:52, 66). Yet denominations that say that miracles are a necessity in the ministry today, and that preaching is not enough, abound. If you take a careful look, you will find that in the Bible, miracles did not lead to conversions. Yet a modern church that promotes itself as a miracles church will usually have a far greater following, temporary as that might be, than a church that focuses on the teaching and preaching of the gospel.

The real purpose of miracles is hard for people to understand, because miracles can seem so exciting in and of themselves. But they were used by God to authenticate, corroborate, and substantiate the gospel ministry of Jesus and his apostles. They were not meant to be the staple of the Christian church for the rest of time. In Hebrews 2:3–4 it says that we must be very careful if we neglect the great salvation of Christ, "which was confirmed" to the first generation of Christians by "signs, wonders and various miracles." The miracles were primarily for them. This passing away of the necessity of the miracle does not mean that God can't do miracles any longer. It only means that the need for them no longer exists, because their purpose is fulfilled. The apostolic record has become the means to bring people to Jesus Christ.

## Prophecy

In the sixth place, there is the gift of prophecy. This term is mentioned in one way or another about twenty-two times in 1 Corinthians 11–14. It comes from the word *prophēmi,* which means "before speak," or "to speak before," is understood by most people to mean "to speak before the time." This is not accurate. Its main meaning is "to speak *before an audience,"* not *"before the time."* The noun *prophets* refers to individuals who speak the truth to others. The prophetic office is of such significance that the church is built upon the "foundation of the apostles and prophets." Where prophets spoke divine revelation, which became the corpus of the Scriptures, we can say that this function of the prophetic office is closed, that prophecy in this sense has ceased, because the final revelatory Word of Christ is spoken. As Hebrews 1:1 says, "In the past God spoke to our forefathers through the prophets . . . , but in these last days he has spoken" (the aorist tense of "has spoken" would mean "finally, fully and definitively").

The final prophetic word of revelation is recorded for us, but does this mean that prophecy as a gift has ceased? The answer is a resounding no, because the fundamental idea of prophecy is the Spirit-derived capacity of a person to proclaim the truth of the Word of God to other people. As the Bible says in 1 Corinthians 14:3, "Everyone who prophesies speaks to men for their strengthening." Whether this is the word of the past ("all things I have said"), the words of the present ("I am with you"), or the future ("I will never leave you" or "I am coming again"), this is the prophetic Word. It can also be understood in a very pastoral sense. When we read of prophecy in 1 Corinthians 14:3, it is the prophet speaking in ways which strengthen, encourage, and comfort the people.

As a pastor, my ministry must be prophetic, which means that my most vital role is to boldly proclaim the Word of God in truth, for the strengthening, encouraging, and comforting of God's people. The preeminence of prophecy is seen again in 1 Corinthians 14:1, where it says that although you should desire the spiritual gifts, you should especially desire to prophesy, because it is a gift that edifies the entire church.

## DISCERNMENT OF SPIRITS

In the seventh place, there is the gift of discernment of spirits. This is connected to the gift of prophecy, because there is the necessity to make sure that the prophetic ministry is completely biblical. This demands the gift of discernment, which helps the people of God know whether a supposed prophetic word is truly from God or not. Just because someone says, "I am a prophet," or "I have a prophetic message," does not mean that this word is consistent with the Word of God. The Scriptures teach in 1 Corinthians 14:29, "Two or three prophets should speak, and the others should weigh carefully what is said [discern]." The word *discern* is not a common word in the New Testament. It is used in only two other places. In Romans 14:1 it says, "Accept him whose faith is weak, without passing judgment on disputable matters." Here discernment is translated as "passing judgment." There are times when such a discerning judgment against a brother is to be withheld in areas that are disputable, such as the celebration of Old Testament feast days and other ceremonial requirements of the Old Testament law.

In Hebrews 5:14, he speaks of the mature who "have trained themselves to distinguish between good and evil." In the Christian life, this gift of discernment is open to all who discipline themselves to distinguish between good and evil. When people don't train themselves, you hear from them that they never know what to believe. One day they believe this doctrine, and the next day they believe the opposite. This is not a knowledgeable flexibility but an immature nondiscernment that is a blight against deep Christian growth. All of us must desire to be discerning good from evil. The failure of this in the garden of Eden led to the entrance of sin into the race. It should be clear for all of us to see just how serious the consequences are when discernment is lacking.

The gifts are divided among the congregation. One person has one gift, while someone else may discover that he has several. Develop them. Make sure to use them at every opportunity. The church isn't nursery school. You don't have to wait to be invited to use a gift. You don't need an office to use a gift. Use your gift whenever and wherever you can.

We live in an age in which Christians lust after experience, desiring more and more visibly manifested gifts. The followers of Jesus Christ can be truly distinctive people only as we seek instead to minister and serve. It may not be flashy, but it may be the very thing another brother or sister needs for spiritual comfort and nurture for a deeply hurting soul. No one else may ever see or know, but God sees. God is pleased with every believer who quietly and faithfully uses all he has for him.

The life of gifted servanthood comes from the work of the Spirit in us. It is not from some determination to be gifted that our gifts flow. It is not from our most passionate efforts that our gifts flow. It is from the grace of God. In the flesh it is impossible to please God—it is impossible to manifest these mighty works of God. It is all of grace, from the receiving, to the using of anything we have and anything we are.

We should focus on what is permanent for the people of God. We should focus on those gifts that continue through this age. By that I mean that some gifts have ceased. The miracles and healings have ceased to be given as a gift. The reason is because they have served their purpose. They authenticated the claims of the gospel. They authenticated the deity of Jesus. They authenticated the apostolic office. When the need for the sign ceased, the gift was no longer given. First Corinthians 13 spoke about this when it said that certain of the gifts would cease. I am afraid that many people don't take that statement seriously. The readers of this book should. We should focus on what is permanent—what abides for the church today. Of course God can choose to heal and do miracles as he wills, but as gifts, these activities have ceased.

First Corinthians 12:11 teaches that "all these are the work of one and the same Spirit." The word for "work" is *energei*. The Spirit "energizes" us with these various gifts, as he directs his church. In a Spirit-energized church, there is unity. We are, as 1 Corinthians 12:13 says, "one body." We are "indispensable" to one another (v. 22), honoring one another (v. 24), compassionate to one another (v. 26), finding our place in the body (v. 28), and desiring what's best for the body (v. 31). It is the Spirit who brings all this to pass.

When our lives are energized by the Spirit, we see all things differently. The gifts should never become a basis for bickering, quarreling, and infighting in the church. The gifts are not given by God against us, but for us! When we turn the gifts into a carnival sideshow, we are living a carnal, sub-Christian life that resembles the confusion in the Corinthian church rather than displaying the glory intended to be displayed by a committed and consecrated body of believers. We must seek after Christ in all his fullness. We must focus on the completed work of Christ. We must use all that we are and all that we have to bring others to Christ—not to bring them to a confusion that a carnal view of the gifts presents but to the Christ of sacrifice, love, and compassion. Our motto should be the words of Paul in this section, "The most excellent way."

**A**s a young Christian, I attended a Bible study where the teacher asked me if I had the Holy Spirit. Then she told me that I didn't have the Holy Spirit if I didn't speak in tongues. She went on to explain that the baptism of the Holy Spirit always followed salvation and was always accompanied by speaking in tongues. I was deeply concerned that I was not a complete Christian until I could get this so-called second blessing. This became a spiritual nightmare, one that is faced by countless Christians every day as they are confronted by well-meaning but theologically dangerous Christians who treat them as second-rate believers until they get this postconversion blessing. They are led to believe that this will make their Christian experience something more substantial. This is the Pentecostal position, the position believed by a very large segment of Protestantism. The most helpful passage in the Bible to deal with this concern is in 1 Corinthians 12. In this text we learn who gives the Holy Spirit, to whom the Holy Spirit is given, how the Holy Spirit is given, when the

> ### 1 CORINTHIANS 12:12-13
>
> [12]The body is a unit, though it is made up of many parts; and though all its parts are many, they form one body. So it is with Christ. [13]For we were all baptized by one Spirit into one body—whether Jews or Greeks, slave or free—and we were all given the one Spirit to drink.

Holy Spirit is given, why the Holy Spirit is given, and how we know when the Holy Spirit is given. Amazingly, this controversial issue is resolved in 1 Corinthians 12:12–13.

This first letter to the Corinthian church deals with one problem after another, one excess upon another, and one abuse after another. We have studied some issues in the past chapters: sexual immorality, divorce, lawsuits, divisions, and more. In 1 Corinthians 12, we come to what is at the heart of Christian fellowship, our oneness in Christ. We as believers are granted eternal life, indwelt by the Holy Spirit, and made into one body in which the Lord dwells. In verses 12 and 13, the theology that undergirds this fellowship and unity is mentioned. It is the baptism of the Holy Spirit. John said in Matthew 3:11 that it is accomplished by Jesus, "He will baptize you with the Holy Spirit." It is not the Holy Spirit who baptizes anyone. It is Christ. Paul speaks of this baptism as the possession of the entire body of Christ. All who belong to Jesus Christ are baptized by him with the Holy Spirit.

This is not the sole possession of some superspiritual Christians who after their conversions received a subsequent blessing, but "we were all baptized by one Spirit into one body." "Baptized by one Spirit" refers to the corporate nature of the Spirit baptism. On Pentecost, it was not a select group of believers who were baptized with the Spirit—it was the entire body, that is, the church. The baptism of the Holy Spirit was a reality for Peter, who had previously denied Jesus Christ. It was a possession of Paul, who had formerly persecuted the church. It was the possession of the woman who had been forgiven much sin. It was the possession of the 120 believers who had all gathered together in one place. These were men and women who had their pride and arrogance ripped from them as they realized their folly in battling against God. These were men and women who saw the fulfillment of the prophet Joel, "I will pour out my Spirit on all people. Your sons and your daughters shall prophesy." Following their baptism with the Spirit, they became vessels that were usable by God. God did a mighty work through them, and we also are those vessels who possess the Spirit and are regenerated so that he can work in us.

As the Scriptures teach, we must not quench the Spirit. We must remember that the Spirit is given to humble us before an all-powerful God, he is given to lead us into all the truth, and he is given to teach us all things about Jesus Christ. The Spirit is given to us so that we would, deep in our being, recall and embrace the great things that God has done in saving a people for himself. The wonders he accomplished were not because of who John and James and Peter and Paul were but in spite of who they were. God used them as they made themselves available to him.

From the beginning we read, "After giving instructions through the Holy Spirit" (Acts 1:2). These are marching orders. This is his army, and he has given marching orders to his people. These orders are to be obeyed. We are able to obey because we are a converted, Spirit-baptized people. He teaches us

his purpose, to show us how this world has been, and how it is
to be, turned upside down for Jesus Christ. That is, a universal
revolution is taking place in which people from every tribe and
tongue and nation are being won for Jesus. In the Book of Acts
people asked, "What is it about these people? How can those
who are so few in number, with no weapons, with no authority,
turn the world upside down?" How did they do this? Only because they were a converted, Spirit-baptized people. They were
filled with the Spirit of God. We must never forget that the baptism with the Holy Spirit is life-changing. It is a reality that is
foundational to the proper functioning of the body of Christ.

We must first understand the meaning of baptism with the
Holy Spirit. Simply put, it is his Spirit, powerfully enabling us
to live godly lives and fulfill the Great Commission. Spirit-bap-
tism power is indeed necessary to be a man or woman of God
and be that witness. But it is a power, we must remember, not
for entertainment or enjoyment. It is a power for living and for
witness. The Scriptures do not teach us that there are Christians who are Spirit-baptized versus Christians who are not
Spirit-baptized. In Acts 2 we learn that the whole church is a
Spirit-baptized church. Here in 1 Corinthians 12, we also see
in the clearest fashion that this baptism has to do with the
church as a whole. It is the church that is to be baptized in,
with, and by the Spirit of God. There are not two churches in
Christendom, a Spirit-baptized church and a non-Spirit-bap-
tized church. Although the Spirit came upon the church cor-
porately on Pentecost, now every time someone comes to
believe savingly in Christ, that person receives the baptism of
the Holy Spirit and is incorporated into the body of Christ.

Think for a moment about what you believe are the main
components of a Spirit-baptized life. Would it be speaking in

tongues, producing miracles, signs, or wonders? In Acts 1, where we read that the believers received the baptism of the Holy Spirit, we see clearly what accompanied that baptism. They had power to be witnesses! This was undergirded by a deep grounding in the Word of God and prayer. These are the basic realities of a Spirit-baptized life.

This first component is power. In Acts 1:8, we read, "You will receive power when the Holy Spirit comes on you." What was the goal of that power? We continue reading, "and you will be my witnesses." The core of this power experience is a prayer-filled life. "These all joined together constantly in prayer" (Acts 1:14), waiting for the marching orders. Peter stood up and said, "The Scripture had to be fulfilled." The Holy Spirit was teaching him that all the confusion of a horrible betrayal and suffering death by Jesus were exactly what had been written in the Scriptures. Their marching orders, their power, and their prayers were all tied to the Word of God. The word *dynamis,* which enters the English language as the word *dynamite,* refers to the power that was given to them by God. These were people who were turned into living dynamite, spiritually speaking. They were power-filled, explosive people. That's how they were able to turn the world upside down. It wasn't because they were intellectually superior. It wasn't because they were morally superior. Just think about these Corinthians and the immorality that characterized them. The church, in spite of its sins, which are continually being dealt with and cleansed, is empowered by the living and true God. When we let ourselves be dynamite for God, we advance his kingdom.

Power is one of the key motivations of people the world over. That's why this dynamite, this power, is so deadly and dangerous when used by the wrong people in the wrong way.

Of course, it is only an imitation when used falsely. A good example of this is Simon Magnus. He saw the power of the apostles in Acts 8:9–25. He said, "I want it! How much does it cost? You name your price. I'll give every cent I've got" (author's paraphrase). Peter responded, "Take your money and perish with it, if you think you can purchase the gift of God." Generation after generation of false teachers have quested after power and attempted to use the church to achieve it. But the power that is given to the people of God is a power that is in opposition to the power of the world. The Scriptures teach, "'Not by might, nor by power, but by my Spirit,' says the LORD Almighty" (Zech. 4:6).

We are not to desire the world's power. We are to humbly submit ourselves to God's power and remember that it is a dynamite that reveals God, not ourselves. The power that Peter and Paul displayed pointed to Jesus. When people tried to worship Paul as a god, he did not let them. When Jesus was embroiled in tremendous controversy over his casting out of demons, he looked at the people and said, "But if I drive out demons by the Spirit of God, then the kingdom of God has come upon you" (Matt. 12:28). The signs and the wonders were displayed so that you would know that the kingdom of God has come. We are empowered to be ready in season and out of season to preach the kingdom of God—not ourselves and what we can do but who Jesus Christ is and what he can do.

We are Spirit-baptized and empowered for witness. Witness is the ultimate, essential ingredient that advances the cause of Christ and his church. Acts 1:8 says, "You will receive power when the Holy Spirit comes on you, and you will be my witnesses." Power and witness are inextricably linked together. You cannot break them. The Greek word for witness is *martyr.*

It referred to an individual who brought a legal declaration of first-hand information. Later it came to mean someone who spoke for Christ and was killed for it. Luke quoted Jesus, "You are witnesses of these things" (Luke 24:48). The three aspects of this witness were mentioned above.

First, *the Scriptures had to be fulfilled* (Luke 24:44). One time when I shared the gospel, the fact that most affected the person with whom I was sharing was my testimony that I came to Christ through the Old Testament, which was fulfilled in Christ. The first thing to remember in your witness is to use the Old Testament, for the Old Testament Scriptures had to be fulfilled. Everything that Jesus did was in fulfillment of the Old Testament Scriptures.

Second, the Scriptures had to be fulfilled in the *death and resurrection of Jesus Christ* (Luke 24:46). This is the center of our faith and hope. Jesus died in our place and rose for us. We read in the Scriptures that if we believe he rose for us, we too will rise together with him. It is our hope. It is our witness. We speak to people who are given over to death and who expect nothing in a zero-expectation generation. Young people growing up today expect nothing. They have no real hope for the future. Our witness is that there is hope and life. There is eternal life through the death and resurrection of Jesus Christ. This fulfills what is written in the Scriptures.

Third, *we proclaim repentance and forgiveness of sins* (Luke 24:47). Why do we need Christ? We need Christ to be our sin-bearer, because we are all sinners. No matter what benevolences we do, no matter how good we are, no matter how gracious and kind we might be, we are in our sin, unless that sin is paid for. The proclamation is that in Christ, there is forgiveness of sins. There is redemption. There is pardon. There is repentance. There is a complete salvation. So remember that the fulfillment of the Scriptures in the death and resurrection of Jesus Christ, and the proclamation of repentance and forgiveness of sins, are the essentials of a Spirit-baptized witness.

We see the connection between our power and witness early in Romans 1:16, where Paul said, "I am not ashamed of the gospel, for it is the power of God for salvation for everyone who believes." In 1 Corinthians 1:18 it is written, "The message of the cross is foolishness to those who are perishing, but to us who are being saved it is the power of God." Power and witness are joined in salvation. When you witness, you're bringing the saving work of God in Jesus Christ. What it also brought the early church was death. That witness was spoken to a hostile government. That witness was spoken to a hostile world. That witness, empowered as it was by the Spirit of God, brought antagonism and rage. It is amazing that a handful of people could so upset the greatest empire in the history of the world. The empire had to systematically attempt to annihilate them because they couldn't be intimidated. These Christians said, "You decide what you're going to do to us, but we must continue speaking what we have seen and heard" (see Acts 4:20). They never shut up, even unto death.

We are embarrassed to witness even when there are no consequences. Maybe we say to ourselves, "When the stakes are really high, then I will be able to do it. Then I will be willing, then I know I will be brave." But the truth is that whoever is not brave or faithful with the little things is not going to be brave or faithful when there are greater things at stake. If you can't be faithful when only your pride is at stake and someone looks at you as some kind of fanatic or fundamentalist, how are you going to be faithful when all it would take to save yourself from physical harm would be a little compromise in denying Jesus? I urge you, when you have the opportunity for witness, take it. Take that death to self, so that if in God's providence a greater sacrifice is demanded one day, you will be ready. You will be able. You will be willing. You will be empowered to stand even unto death as those witnesses/martyrs stood for Jesus.

The foundation of the witness of our Spirit-baptized life has to come from the Scriptures. What we have to share is not extrabiblical revelation. It is not the so-called revelation that any person expresses, even if that person says, "Thus says the Lord," and "Here's what you're supposed to do." Reply, "Show me from the Bible." Say, "What the Bible says is our standard. That is our norm. That is our rule. That is our book—the Word of the living God." This will keep you from being exploited or manipulated. It is God's Word that is foundational. Even Jesus, when he faced the devil, responded to him, "Man does not live on bread alone, but on every word that comes from the mouth of God" (Matt. 4:4). That is our food. That is our nutrition. That is our sustenance, just as it was for Jesus.

The significance of living a Spirit-baptized life is clear.

First, *the Spirit-baptized life is a life of prayer.* "They all joined together constantly in prayer" (Acts 1:14). If we want to be a Spirit-baptized church, then we should ask, "Are we filled with prayer?" What is your prayer life like? Every Christian is to be continually devoted to prayer, continually seeking communion and fellowship with God. We should be prayerful that every interaction is blessed by him and led by him. Then he will direct us to people who are being prepared by him for our witness. If we are not prayerful at all times, we are going to be caught off guard. We are going to be lulled with a false sense of complacency and security when we should be vigilant, sober, on guard. What then is the Spirit-baptized life? It is a life of power and witness, molded by the Word of the Living God, undergirded by a life continually given over to prayer.

Second, because of our conversion and baptism with the Holy Spirit, *we are all one in Christ* (1 Cor. 12:12). Any striving should be for unity in the body. This doesn't mean that we compromise truth but only that we are careful to cultivate oneness and not division, even as we recognize our differences. We remember that all true believers are baptized with one Spirit.

Third, salvation and Holy Spirit baptism give us *"everything we need for life and godliness"* (2 Peter 1:3). We don't need subsequent blessings! We already have been blessed more than we can ever imagine. We simply have to joyfully and gratefully use everything we have been given.

Fourth, *the barriers between us are down.* This passage says it all. With the baptism of the Holy Spirit, we are unified, whether we are slave or free, Jew or Gentile, male or female (Gal. 3:28). Groups that formerly warred against each other have put away their weapons and now rejoice in their oneness in Christ. This is the amazing and incomprehensible work of the Holy Spirit.

You should seek that Spirit-baptized, Spirit-filled life. That is, seek a power-filled life of witness and love for Christ! To seek this life is to live out what we already have. It is not for some higher-level Christians—it is for all of us. The text says, "We were all baptized by one Spirit into one body." It is a life that seeks to maximize every opportunity to witness for Jesus Christ, with power. It doesn't wait for future opportunities—it takes the opportunities we have now. Take hold of the power that has been given to you by joining the faithful line of martyrs/witnesses, whose power-filled testimony was used by God to change the world!

n the church at Corinth one issue was causing more confusion than almost any other—the question of speaking
in tongues. This gift was given on Pentecost, when God
miraculously enabled the entire church to speak languages
that they did not know. We read, "All of them . . . began to
speak in other tongues" (Acts 2:4). What was the Spirit of God
saying to his people at that time? This blessing caused confusion then. In fact, the first response to the manifestation of
this gift was, "What does this mean?" (Acts 2:12). There is no
less confusion today.

What was the day of Pentecost? Why is it such a meaningful event for the people of God? In the Old Testament,
God's people had three yearly celebrations. One of them was
the Day of Firstfruits, which fell on the fiftieth day after the
consecration of the harvest season. Thus it was called Pentecost, or fiftieth day. It celebrated the completion of the grain
harvest, and the firstfruits of the wheat were presented to the
Lord. What a picture for the Pentecost celebration in Acts!

### *1 CORINTHIANS 14:1-26*

[1]Follow the way of love and eagerly desire spiritual gifts, especially the gift of prophecy. [2]For anyone who speaks in a tongue does not speak to men but to God. Indeed, no one understands him; he utters mysteries with his spirit. [3]But everyone who prophesies speaks to men for their strengthening, encouragement and comfort. [4]He who speaks in a tongue edifies himself, but he who prophesies edifies the church. [5]I would like every one of you to speak in tongues, but I would rather have you prophesy. He who prophesies is greater than one who speaks in tongues, unless he interprets, so that the church may be edified.

[6]Now, brothers, if I come to you and speak in tongues, what good will I be to you, unless I bring you some revelation or knowledge or prophecy or word of instruction? [7]Even in the case of lifeless things that make sounds, such as the flute or harp, how will anyone know what tune is being played unless there is a distinction in the notes? [8]Again, if the trumpet does not sound a clear call, who will get ready for battle? [9]So it is with you. Unless you speak intelligible words with your tongue, how will anyone know what you are saying? You will just be speaking into the air. [10]Undoubtedly there are all sorts of languages in the world, yet none of them is without meaning. [11]If then I do not grasp the meaning of what someone is saying, I am a foreigner to the speaker, and he is a foreigner to me. [12]So it is with you. Since you are eager to have spiritual gifts, try to excel in gifts that build up the church.

¹³For this reason anyone who speaks in a tongue should pray that he may interpret what he says. ¹⁴For if I pray in a tongue, my spirit prays, but my mind is unfruitful. ¹⁵So what shall I do? I will pray with my spirit, but I will also pray with my mind; I will sing with my spirit, but I will also sing with my mind. ¹⁶If you are praising God with your spirit, how can one who finds himself among those who do not understand say "Amen" to your thanksgiving, since he does not know what you are saying? ¹⁷You may be giving thanks well enough, but the other man is not edified.

¹⁸I thank God that I speak in tongues more than all of you. ¹⁹But in the church I would rather speak five intelligible words to instruct others than ten thousand words in a tongue.

²⁰Brothers, stop thinking like children. In regard to evil be infants, but in your thinking be adults. ²¹In the Law it is written:

> Through men of strange tongues
>    and through the lips of foreigners
> I will speak to this people,
>    but even then they will not listen to me," says
>    the Lord.

²²Tongues, then, are a sign, not for believers but for unbelievers; prophecy, however, is for believers, not for unbelievers. ²³So if the whole church comes together and everyone speaks in tongues, and some who do not un-

> derstand or some unbelievers come in, will they not say that you are out of your mind? 24But if an unbeliever or someone who does not understand comes in while everybody is prophesying, he will be convinced by all that he is a sinner and will be judged by all, 25and the secrets of his heart will be laid bare. So he will fall down and worship God, exclaiming, "God is really among you!"
>
> 26What then shall we say, brothers? When you come together, everyone has a hymn, or a word of instruction, a revelation, a tongue or an interpretation. All of these must be done for the strengthening of the church.

God was presenting the firstfruits of his harvest of believers from all over the world!

What did the languages have to do with what God was communicating? Let's think back to the early times of the Old Testament, when there was only one language. What a satisfying thing it must have been to communicate with anyone in the world. Imagine what could have been accomplished. People at that time did have great plans, but their plans turned against God. They began building the tower of Babel in defiance of his rule. The way God foiled those plans and brought judgment was by confusing the people's languages. They could no longer communicate!

Now let's travel forward from this event to the time of Isaiah, where the negative impact of diverse languages is also presented. "With foreign lips and strange tongues God will speak to this people, to whom he said, 'This is the resting place, let the weary have rest'; and, 'this is the place of repose'; but they would not listen" (Isa. 28:11–12). This passage was declaring judgment on Israel because of its continued apostasy. Isaiah was predicting the impending invasion of Assyria and Israel's resulting captivity, as well as the future invasion by Babylon of Judah, resulting in God's judgment and their final captivity. He said, "You will hear men, who are going to be your conquerors, speaking in languages you will not understand. They will be your captors. When you hear those incomprehensible languages, then know that my judgment has come." This passage was dealing with the terrible judgment of God, saying that if you hear unintelligible speech in the assembly, judgment has come!

Jesus warned that Jerusalem would be destroyed. He said the people would be led captive into all the nations by men of other tongues. In fulfillment of that prophecy, Titus destroyed the city of Jerusalem in A.D. 70 and dispersed the Jews throughout all the nations.

Israel knew that tongues meant judgment. When Israel heard other languages in the assembly, this was a sign of God's judgment. The languages that unbelieving Israel heard at Pentecost were a sign of judgment on them. Just as God was bringing a harvest of salvation—those who believed—so also he was pronouncing judgment on those who rejected Christ the Savior.

This was the commencement of the last days. Hebrews 1:1 says, "in these last days," and this is the message of these last days. It is the message that God brought full and final redemption from sin in the person of his Son, Jesus Christ. What happened on Pentecost was that each person heard this great redemptive work of God in his own language! The message came this way because the New Testament was not yet written, and God used a new way to bring this final message.

It was a way that the Jewish people in particular would notice. The church was speaking foreign languages, something that was indisputably miraculous. The Jews from every nation under heaven could now know that what had taken place in Jesus was undoubtedly the work of God, a work that they should embrace. This work would be fully explained when the New Testament was completed. Should they have been surprised? Of course not! This is exactly what Joel prophesied, as Peter stated, "What you're hearing is what was spoken of through the prophet Joel."

We can refer to the days of Moses to contrast God's judgment in history and his salvation as recorded in the Book of Acts. While Moses was on the mountain of God receiving the tablets with the commandments, the people of God were waiting for him in the camp. The people tired of waiting for Moses, who was gone for forty days, and they made the golden calf with Aaron. Then they celebrated around this idol. When Moses came down from the mountain, he was furious with Aaron and the people. On this first fiftieth-day celebration in the time of the Old Covenant, about three thousand men were judged for their wickedness and put to death. On the first celebration of Pentecost in the New Covenant, as we read in Acts, about three thousand people received salvation and were saved from the judgment of God.

## An Apostolic Sign

Tongues were connected primarily with the apostolic office. They directly bore witness to the resurrected Christ. That's why Paul said in 1 Corinthians 14:22 that "tongues, then, are a sign." They were a sign that validated the ministry of Christ. They were a sign as well of the apostolic office, which itself validated the ministry of Christ.

The gift ceased when it had served its purpose, which was to validate the life and ministry of Christ during the time when the New Testament Scriptures were being compiled. Although the scope of tongues and the usage of tongues was broader than the apostles, the gift was intimately connected with their ministry, which was a ministry designed to bring prophetic revelation. As Acts 2:11 teaches, it was to be the new revelation of the mighty deeds of God in Jesus Christ. Tongues, like the apostles who spoke those tongues, were for the foundation of the early church. So then tongues were withdrawn from the life of the church, along with revelatory prophecy and any other foundational gifts, when the church was established. These signs were bound up with the presence of the apostles at that time when New Testament revelation had not yet either been fully given to the church or fully received by the church.

In summary, the purposes of this gift were to be an authenticating sign of the infant church, an authenticating sign of the apostles, and a sign of the judgment to come on Israel. With the passing away of the theocracy, that is, the nation of Israel, and the apostles, the sign as well passed away. As Paul said in 1 Corinthians 13:8, "Tongues . . . will be stilled." He used a verb that means that tongues shall cease in and of themselves, the only question being when. That time of cessation is A.D. 70.

Languages have meaning. In 1 Corinthians 14:10–11, Paul declared, "There are all sorts of languages in the world, yet none of them is without meaning." He added, "If then I do not grasp the meaning of what someone is saying, I am a foreigner to the speaker, and he is a foreigner to me." Paul was saying that every language in the world has meaning. What a blessing that is, because God created language so that we could interact with each other and understand one another.

Paul spoke of foreigners in 1 Corinthians 14:21. He pointed out that foreigners don't babble—they speak languages. The languages they speak sound like babbling only to those who don't know them. Furthermore, everyone speaks a foreign language—to those who don't know their language.

Even angels, speaking in the Scriptures, always spoke in the language of the person they addressed. They never spoke an unintelligible language. The tongues of angels remain until the end, the understandable languages of humankind. There is no indication anywhere in the Scriptures that angels ever spoke any language that was not understandable or that a language they use in heaven is unintelligible language. When the verse says, "If I speak in the tongues of men and of angels," it does not promote the idea that angels speak a heavenly, incomprehensible language. Rather, the verse supports the scriptural pattern of intelligible speech by men *and* angels. It indicates that men and angels are alike when it comes to communication—both use languages to communicate and understand one another.

## INTELLIGIBLE LANGUAGE

Exactly what happened on Pentecost? This is the first line of confusion for most Christians. Acts 2:4 states, "All of them were filled with the Holy Spirit and began to speak in other tongues as the Spirit enabled them." Acts 2:6 says, "When they heard this sound, a crowd came together in bewilderment, because each one *heard them speaking in his own language.*" In

Acts 2:8 they asked, "Then how is it that each of us hears them in his own native language?" In Acts 2:11 it says, "We hear them declaring the wonders of God in our own tongues!"

The question is, Was this event on Pentecost the beginning of what we now see practiced regularly in Pentecostal and charismatic churches? Is that situation, this situation? In Acts the people did not hear language they could not understand. They heard the Word of God, the mighty deeds of God, each in his own language.

We are called to worship God with our minds. Jesus said in Matthew 22:37, "Love the Lord your God with all your heart and with all your soul and with all your mind." This condemns worship activity that is mindless. The way we love the Lord is different from the way the eastern religious worshipers love their idols, which is to worship by emptying their minds. In biblical religion, we are always to love God with all our minds.

The pattern of New Testament worship is the synagogue. After God's people in the Old Testament returned from Babylon, they no longer had the temple worship with its sacrifices. They gathered weekly in the synagogue to worship. Here they sang psalms, prayed, read the Scriptures, and heard expositions of the Scriptures. The early church continued this pattern of worship when they met from house to house. The church is even called the synagogue in one place. In James 2:2 we read, "If a man comes into your meeting . . ." That word *meeting* or *assembly* obviously refers to the church, because the assembly is the gathering of the people of God. Yet the word in the Greek from which it is translated is the word *synagogue*. That is how close the connection was between the Old Covenant synagogue and the New Covenant church. Likewise, the purpose for our modern-day churches to gather on the Lord's day is to worship. We worship to learn of God and to be edified about the person and character of God. Our worship is in a framework of intelligibility and thoughtfulness.

How do we prefer that other people communicate with us? We value communication that we can understand, and we sympathize with those who are limited. Isn't it a handicap, even in the case of little children who are developing their abilities, to be limited in mind or speaking ability? It is never something positive. In fact, we even correct the *pronunciation* of our children, telling them to "enunciate." (Could these parents be the same people who believe that God wants to hear their unintelligible utterances?) How does God want us to communicate with him? He wants us to interact to the best of our abilities. At the beginning of creation, he communicated with the first people he created, Adam and Eve. They walked and talked in the garden together, most certainly expressing themselves in ways clearly understood. Throughout the Scriptures, God's people spoke to him with words that even we can understand, and God also interacted with them understandably. Jesus taught his people how to pray in the Lord's Prayer, and it is clear from the pattern he gave us that the communication he wants from us is to be intelligible and rational. He gave us language so that we can clearly express our adoration for him and our needs to him.

The text commands God's people to "stop thinking like children," which is what making unintelligible utterances as a standard for prayer life is doing. They were children in their understanding. As a church they had never grown up, because they didn't think. Instead, they should have had minds that were perfect, or mature, or at the very least adult. To babble on as they were doing was to be like infants. In fact, a Pentecostal woman told me that her two-year-old daughter spoke in tongues. When I asked her how she could possibly know that, she immediately responded that she knew because her daughter "babbled." Paul was saying, "Don't think like this. This is childish. This is foolish."

Only in their knowledge of evil should believers be children. That is, they should have no experiential knowledge of evil. In all the rest of their thinking, including understanding this issue, their thinking and their experiential knowledge should be mature. Therefore, the Corinthians' self-absorption with this gift, their twisting of this gift into something self-centered and nonedifying for the rest of the body, was in effect evil. What they were doing was not just an error. It was evil. It was an evil that had to be stopped, so that in relationship to the truth, they could grow up.

When Paul spoke of languages without meaning in 1 Corinthians 14:11, the word translated "meaning" in the Greek is *dynamis*. Literally then, the phrase is "languages without power." He was saying that the ecstatic, unintelligible speech of the Corinthians was powerless, because it was meaningless. What took place in Corinth, and what now occurs in our century in charismatic churches, is without power. Just like the Pentecostal woman with the two-year-old daughter who babbled, it is infantile and powerless. The situation is the same for modern congregations with ecstatic utterances as it was with the congregation in Corinth. These are churches without power.

We should also understand the only two other biblical occurrences of what took place on Pentecost. Both of these instances are also in the Book of Acts. The first, in Acts 10, concerns Cornelius, a Roman centurion. He was a God-fearer, or a proselyte to Judaism. When the household of Cornelius believed the truth, they exercised the identical gift found in Acts 2. Peter saw this and responded that the Gentiles needed to be included in the church, because what happened to them is exactly what happened to the church on Pentecost. How much earlier had that happened? Was Pentecost a few days or weeks previous to the day that Cornelius's household received the gift of the Holy Spirit? Was it six months before? It had been eight years before! He didn't say, "Brothers, this is what we do all the time." It was something distinctive, as the Word of God had been brought to the Jews and now was also brought to the Gentiles, eight years later! Peter compared the situation of Cornelius with Pentecost. The idea is simple. As the gospel opened to the Jews on Pentecost, in identical fashion it moved to the Gentiles on the day of Cornelius's conversion.

At Ephesus a third enactment of Pentecost took place. Jewish believers were involved. But this time it was the strict followers of John the Baptist, the religiously pure of the pure. These people were the most perfect Jews in every detail. They had accepted the baptism of John and then learned that their fastidious attachment to Jewish law couldn't save them without Jesus Christ. This encounter was as climactic as Pentecost in Acts 2 or Cornelius's conversion in Acts 10, because it clarified that no matter who you are or what you are, you must come to Christ. They were joined into Christ identically as at Pentecost and Caesarea. In other words, what happened at these three places was not babbling or ecstatic utterances. The tongues they spoke were the clearly understood languages of the listeners, so that the mighty deeds of God would be revealed to the church, Jewish and Gentile, from the uttermost parts of the earth. Again, what was being declared by their tongues? "The wonders of God" (Acts 2:11), with complete understanding.

The only other place in the Bible that deals with speaking in tongues is 1 Corinthians. It is amazing that such a large segment of evangelical Christians should make the Corinthian disaster the standard of behavior, and even the highest level of supposed piety, for the church. Is there a new meaning for the term that is used here in Corinthians? No, the word is exactly the same word that is used in Acts. Yet this word is given a totally different meaning when it is used to justify so-called Pentecostalism. *Glōssalalia* means "language." In every instance that biblical tongues occur, the word *glōssa* is used. There is no linguistic or exegetical justification for changing the meaning of the word from "languages that were understood" to "ecstatic utterances," which is what Pentecostals and charismatics routinely do. The Bible gives a definition of tongues in terms of understandable languages and in no place states a redefinition.

## EDIFYING WORSHIP

Furthermore, the passage says, "Tongues, then, are a sign" (1 Cor. 14:22). This is central to the problem in Corinth, because we must note *to whom* they are a sign. "Tongues are a sign, not for believers but for unbelievers." Tongues are not to be a sign to Christians but to those who do not believe. First Corinthians 14:22 in the Greek text opens with the words "so then," which means that verse 22 makes an argument that hinges on verse 21. Verse 21 says, "Through men of strange tongues and through the lips of foreigners, I will speak to this people, but even then they will not listen to me" (quoting Isa. 28:11–12). Then Paul followed with, "Tongues, then, are a sign, not for believers but for unbelievers."

Do we reach the lost with tongues speaking? The idea in 1 Corinthians 14:16 is that what the Corinthians were doing in their worship was an abomination to any visitors. He was saying that any visitor who was ignorant of what was going on, who had come and had no reason to expect such mindless behavior, would never be able to say "Amen" (or "I agree") to a congregation full of mindless babblers.

The hallmark of our worship is edification, and Paul said, "This is not taking place." He concluded in this section that he would rather speak five intelligible words than myriads of words. The expression he employed was not "ten thousand," but literally the highest figure he could give, which is translated ten thousands of ten thousands, or millions. Once again he was showing his commitment to the Word of God and the enduring edification of the church.

Some people try to justify the idea that there are two kinds of tongues, those of the Book of Acts and those for private edification. What they don't acknowledge is that Paul, in addressing private ecstatic utterances, never endorsed them but strongly rebuked them. He never suggested that they are the standard for the church. They are to be viewed as an aberration from the truth. Paul's words in 1 Corinthians 12–14 have to do with the fact that there is a spiritual disaster happening in the church in Corinth. He was not saying that this is rich, pious worship. In fact, what took place here is astounding, because it is the first time that unknown tongues were spoken in the church. Jesus never did it. The apostles never did it. But the Corinthian church was doing it with a vengeance, and this behavior was what caused Paul's concern. He was dealing with a behavior that did not resemble biblical tongues. Rather, what was going on in Corinth was an entirely different phenomenon from what took place in Acts.

In 1 Corinthians 14:2, Paul made it clear that what the Corinthians were doing brought no edification to the church. When Paul said in 1 Corinthians 14:5 that he would like the whole church to speak in tongues, he was saying that he wanted them to have the real gift, which had not yet fully passed away from the scene. That is, he desired that all of them should be able to speak of the redemptive grace of God in comprehensible languages that they did not understand. But he was most certainly not desiring that they would all be doing what some of them were doing, which edified no one. It left them with the sense that they had been self-edified. He immediately added that his greater desire in the context of real gifts was for them to prophesy, because with prophecy there is always edification for the church.

The essence of the passage is that all things are to be done for edification, not for self-absorption or self-enjoyment. Notice in 1 Corinthians 14:4 that what they were doing was self-edification, which is a contradiction in terms! They should have been concerned with the edification of the brothers and sisters. Again, in verse 5, what they were doing didn't edify the church.

Paul was saying that tongues were being used when nobody present could understand them. That's what the context of this was all about: foreign languages that couldn't be understood. It is not that they could not be understood by anyone, only that in Corinth, there was no understanding because they all spoke Greek. Speaking a foreign tongue edified no one. He illustrated this with a musical example. In 1 Corinthians 14:7–8, he said that there must be variation in music to make it meaningful, or else it is aggravating noise. I learned this lesson firsthand when I was growing up in the Bronx. I wanted to play an instrument, and we had no money for anything, let alone a musical instrument. My mother did say, though, that if I saved my money, I could use it to rent an instrument and take lessons. I rented a trumpet, and every day for about forty-five minutes, I went to my room, opened the windows wide, and played "Three Blind Mice," over and over and over again—until representatives from the entire neighborhood came up to our apartment and said they were going to kill me if I didn't stop. They didn't say that my noise was a higher spiritual reality but that I had better stop, or they were going to kill me because there was no edification in my tune. When that happens in the church, and there is no edification in the indistinguishable noise that is created, people are called the spiritual giants of the Christian faith! They say that this is the second, the highest blessing in Christianity, and everyone who doesn't have it is spiritually dead!

The languages in Acts were given to declare the Word of God and the mighty deeds of God. For those in the generation in which the New Covenant Word had not yet been compiled (remember, what they heard was the mighty works of God in their own, understandable, languages), what they were given in those supernatural speeches was far less than what we have available to us every day in the complete and unabridged Word of God!

Pursue, as 1 Corinthians 14:1 says, the spiritual gifts that are available to the body of Christ today. But most eagerly seek for prophecy, which today is the bringing forth of the Word of God. This is a gift that brings "strengthening, encouragement and comfort" (1 Cor. 14:3). It "edifies the church" (1 Cor. 14:4). "It is greater" because the church is edified (1 Cor. 14:5). Also, 1 Corinthians 14:24 says, it convinces unbelievers of their sins.

Tongues is not on the list of spiritual gifts. A final challenge from this section is that the legitimate gift of tongues is not found in the lists of spiritual gifts in Romans 12:6–8 or Ephesians 4:11. It is only here, apart from the three references in Acts. It is mentioned only in the church in Corinth, a carnal, scandal-filled church. It is mentioned as an aberration that is identically seen in the twentieth-century church. It is an aberration that fills the church precisely because it is easy and mindless.

We are in the strange and biblically untenable position of seeing the church at large enamored with the sign that ceased and avoiding the direct and revealed Word of God. Numerous Pentecostals have told me that they love to come to the congregation where I preach to hear the Word of God, but they love to go to Pentecostal churches for worship, because the experience they have is so "worshipful." How can it be worshipful if the Word of God—the Word that those tongues revealed—is being neglected!

Tongues were given for the opposite reason than what happens in the church today. People are told to speak in tongues to show that they are Spirit-filled Christians. But Paul taught that tongues are a sign of God's judgment against unbelievers. Tongues were a sign of God's impending judgment on unbelieving Israel and were never to be used in the presence of unbelievers in worship because it would only harden them in the rejection of the gospel. That is exactly what was happening in Corinth. Paul said that unbelievers thought the Corinthians were crazy. The question, then, is this: As tongues in Israel demonstrated God's judgment and rejection of them, what significance do tongues have in the New Covenant community? I believe they were meant to be a sign of the ultimate judgment of God and that tongues were the fulfillment of the prophecy reinforced at the birth of Christ, "This child is destined to cause the falling and rising of many in Israel," and to be a sign that they would be rejected.

## EXPERIENCE AND EXCITEMENT

Personal experience is prioritized in our day. Early in the twentieth century, liberalism seemed to uproot belief in the Word of God. What appeared to be left was experience, and it is impossible to argue with experience. The only point of contention is what a particular experience means. In a century of increasing skepticism, people were told that they could have all the experiences they wanted, as long as they kept them private. This brought about the loss of the Word of God, which has led to a truncated gospel, which has resulted in ineffectiveness in reaching a lost world with the saving gospel of Jesus Christ. We are in a spiritual battle in which experience is antithetical to truth. We need to remember that experience is always to be gauged by the barometer of the Word of God. That is the standard for life and experience.

What is the experience of speaking in tongues? Am I denying this experience? Of course not! An experience cannot be denied. I am rejecting the idea that the experience of speaking in tongues is biblical. I am saying that it is a kind of spontaneous, nonconceptual, prevocalization of which every human being is capable. Some of the participants have an amazingly ecstatic experience. Yet none of the activities that are used today to enable people to speak in tongues are mentioned in the Bible.

Prayer is intense work. It takes total concentration. There may be a temptation to make it into a feel-good experience, so that when the hard work of praying becomes tiring, one can babble. But this is not pleasing to God, who wants our prayers intelligible.

Ecstasy, experience, and excitement were what it was all about in Corinth. These elements are as powerful as a narcotic. The experience of having something take over your tongue, as some people describe it, and to have syllables pour out, seemingly beyond your control, is as powerful as a narcotic. That is what Pentecostalism is all about—subjectivity and personally exhilarating, but infantile, experience. A vast proportion of the church is avidly devoted to worship speech that is absolutely not understandable, even to the person who is speaking. That is why Paul wouldn't even come and use the true gift with the Corinthians. As a matter of fact, although Paul said he spoke in tongues more than any of them, he never recorded a single instance of such use on his or anyone else's part.

Those who are devoted to this experience say that doctrine doesn't matter among Christian people when they share a religious experience. They think they have come to something that seems alive, an experience that takes precedence over any doctrinal agreement or even any doctrinal disagreement. Tongues unites the modern charismatic movement, which embraces people from every religious background. This is frightening, because this experience has transcended all doctrinal differences: people who believe in justification by faith and people who don't; people who believe in the deity of Jesus Christ and people who don't; people who believe in the virgin birth, the miracles, the resurrection and the atonement, and people who deny them. In other words, Christians from conservative churches have joined with Roman Catholics and with liberal churches and united in a worship that sends them soaring, even though portions of this one new overarching group have denied central doctrines of the Christian faith. Speaking in tongues has brought unexpected groups together. It has become the great leveler, so that doctrine has become secondary to experience. Secondary is not the right word—the correct word is "inconsequential." It is inconsequential to outbursts of gibberish.

Many non-Christian religious groups today, as well, speak in tongues that are ecstatic, nonunderstandable utterances: Mormons, The Way, Hindus, Muslims, and others. If you went to a worship service of the cult group The Way International, what you would hear is ecstatic utterances exactly as you would hear them in any Pentecostal assembly. Throughout history, it is also recorded that pagan groups spoke with similar ecstatic utterances during their religious ceremonies.

Does any kingdom work occur? Or even any deep communion with God? These are important questions to ask, especially since there is no reason to assume that this is what he told us to do. More importantly, there is the danger of playing with such activity and leaving ourselves open and vulnerable to satanic assaults, which invariably damage the individual and the church. God's people are to be filled with the Spirit in a biblical way, and this passage gives us some guidelines.

1. Each person is given a manifestation of the Spirit for the common good (1 Cor. 12:7).
2. Unity along with diversity of gifts is essential. In other words, there shouldn't be pride, envy, or arrogance. We all have different gifts (1 Cor. 12:5).
3. Our desire must be for the greater and enduring gifts, such as faith, hope, and love (1 Cor. 13:13).

4. Pursue spiritual gifts, but especially prophecy, in which you bring the Word of God, understandably, to people's lives and hearts (1 Cor. 14:1).

5. Do not crave excitement or experience. You'll get them, and you may get more than you bargained for (1 Cor. 14:23).

6. Do not forbid the true manifestation of true spiritual gifts (1 Cor. 14:39–40).

7. In all things, seek the edification of the church, not self-edification. The entire teaching on tongues draws to a close saying that when we come together for worship, whatever we bring and whatever we do must be done for edification. Everything we do should build up one another.

8. Let all be done properly and in order so that Christ will be honored and glorified (1 Cor. 14:40). Paul gave the overarching principle for the worship service when he said that "God is not a God of disorder, but of peace." Everything that is part of our worship reflects the character of God. The disorder and chaos of a Pentecostal service is a contradiction of the character of God. Whenever you see a service where hundreds of people are speaking out at the same time, remember that even when the true gift of tongues existed, Paul told them that only two or three at most could bring a foreign language, and then only if an interpreter was present. The abuses in charismatic churches are against easily understandable commands. When this is the practice, it can never glorify God (1 Cor. 14:33). So when people criticize your church for the kind of worship service characterized as orderly, remember

that order is in keeping with the character of God. He is not a God of confusion.

What does Pentecost in Acts mean to us as believers? It was the commencement of the last days. It was the firstfruits of the harvest of New Covenant believers and a sign of the judgment to come on Israel. The mighty deeds of God in Christ Jesus were heard in the languages of all the people who were listening. The tongues spoken at that occasion and the two other occasions in the New Testament confirmed the inclusion of the Gentiles into the covenant people of God and verified the necessity of joining with the people of God through our Savior, Jesus Christ. The apostles were vindicated and the infant church was authenticated. The sign of tongues accomplished the purposes for which God had intended it, as prophesied in the Old Testament, and ceased as a gift.

How should we as Christians now worship the true and living God? It is no mystery—he tells us how to worship in his written Word, which is available to us. He wants to be worshiped with all of our hearts and souls and minds. He wants to hear the praises of his people who adore him, in every language of the earth. He wants us to worship together with our brothers and sisters, edifying and building up one another, and not living for ourselves. He wants us to use the spiritual gifts he has given us to *that* end. The Holy Spirit, who bestows the gifts on all God's people, enables them to glorify God with their praises and build up his church with love for God's people. That is the blessing of the Spirit-filled lives of the church.

I could subtitle this chapter "Meet Jesus Christ," in response to a movie, *Meet Joe Black,* I saw once on a transatlantic flight. This movie is about a man who came back from the dead in a resurrected (and very good-looking) body and could even grant life to someone whose time for death had come. He had an after-death affair with a beautiful young woman. The movie espouses the kind of life after death that all non-Christians long for—no judgment, no punishment, no pain, and no lostness forever. It satisfies in that way. It is a movie for people who are troubled about the Christian message of eternal judgment for those who reject Jesus Christ, for there is apparent life and abundance without Christ in this film. There is no necessity whatsoever for faith in Christ, and certainly no reason to fear death!

This movie is consistent with a spate of other movies that preach the same theme, for example, the popular *City of Angels.* Some years back there was the hit film *Ghost,* on the same subject. These movies are sermons. Instead of being named

> ### 1 CORINTHIANS 15:20-28
>
> [20]But Christ has indeed been raised from the dead, the firstfruits of those who have fallen asleep. [21]For since death came through a man, the resurrection of the dead comes also through a man. [22]For as in Adam all die, so in Christ all will be made alive. [23]But each in his own turn: Christ, the firstfruits; then, when he comes, those who belong to him. [24]Then the end will come, when he hands over the kingdom to God the Father after he has de-

*Meet Joe Black,* the name could have been *A Beautiful Resurrection without the Need for Jesus Christ.* It is part of a deep and persistent philosophical trend to lull people to the true gospel of the death and resurrection of Jesus Christ and the necessity to trust in Christ alone to be saved and have eternal life.

In 1 Corinthians 15:1–11, we see that the Corinthians believed the gospel, received the gospel, and stood firm in the gospel. We see as well that in this gospel, the resurrection of Jesus Christ is of primary importance. In 1 Corinthians 15:12–19, Paul was amazed that the Corinthians held fast to the faith but denied the resurrection of the dead. The denial of the resurrection of the dead meant that Jesus Christ also was not raised from the dead! As he said in verse 13, "If there is no resurrection of the dead, then not even Christ has been raised." This position ultimately meant that they had believed in vain. "We are to be pitied more than all men" (v. 19). But the matter did not stop there, for if it had stopped at verse 19, it would have been a message of disastrous defeat. It was concluded in verses 20–28. Indeed, it is a note of triumph and

stroyed all dominion, authority and power. [25]For he must reign until he has put all his enemies under his feet. [26]The last enemy to be destroyed is death. [27]For he "has put everything under his feet." Now when it says that "everything" has been put under him, it is clear that this does not include God himself, who put everything under Christ. [28]When he has done this, then the Son himself will be made subject to him who put everything under him, so that God may be all in all.

victory, for the apostle took great pains to affirm the resurrection of Jesus Christ and our resurrection in and with him.

Paul spoke of the certainty of the resurrection of Jesus Christ. This section opens as if the apostle were saying, "You have heard the concern. You know what is involved in the rejection of the resurrection of the dead—you know this means the rejection of the resurrection of Jesus Christ. You know that this ultimately means that you too are lost and hopeless." Knowing this, he declared to God's people the certainty that Jesus is raised from the dead. The apostle took all that had been presented beforehand, giving it, as it were, a cry of deliverance straight from his opening words. Death is no nightmare, because there is resurrection. There is no need to pity those who have trusted Christ. For those who have stood firm, there is no need to fear hell. There is no abyss of utter darkness awaiting those who believe in Jesus Christ, for now Jesus has been raised from the dead. These opening words 1 Corinthians 15:20 present the contrast between the lostness of a world rejecting Christ and the perfect reality of the finished work of Christ.

The apostle used an interesting term to signify Christ's resurrection. Paul called him the "firstfruits," the *aparchē,* a technical word that refers to the first part of a harvest that is connected to all of that particular harvest to follow. Jesus is the firstfruits, then, of a resurrection harvest that must of necessity include all true believers. The resurrection of believers is certain, because the resurrection of Jesus as the firstfruits is certain. Not only was Christ raised from the dead, but he also cannot be separated from all those who have died in him. Paul specifically calls him "the firstfruits of those who have fallen asleep." The idea of sleep is explained in the next words as death. Indeed, the thrust of the text is that the dead in Christ shall all rise, for since death came through a man, life comes through the God-man, Jesus. We who trust in Christ can never be isolated from Christ, nor he from us. We are inseparable. We know that the Scriptures speak this way when they speak of us being in Christ. But here the point is that we are in Christ not only in his death but also in his resurrection!

The resurrection of Jesus Christ is the ultimate victory. In fact, almost every word in this section is a note of certainty and victory. It begins, "But Christ has indeed been raised from the dead" (1 Cor. 15:20). "In Christ all will be made alive" (v. 22). "He must reign until he has put all his enemies under his feet" (v. 25). "He has put everything under his feet" (v. 27). "God [is] all in all" (v. 28). This is a portrait of the most triumphant victory. There is no hesitation. There is no equivocation. This is the reality that all in the early church believed without dispute. This is the triumph—that Christ is alive after a cruel and vicious death. Of course the Corinthian church agreed with that. Their dispute concerned whether *they* were to be raised after death. Here we read, "Christ is . . . the firstfruits of those who have fallen asleep" (v. 20). The destiny of dead believers is triumphantly dealt with here and should silence any controversy. They shall live because he lives!

The argument then seemed to take a pessimistic turn when it said, "in Adam all die" (1 Cor. 15:22), which means that we are all condemned to death in the one representative head of the human race. When he sinned, we were all reckoned sinners in him, and when he died, we died in him. We inherited a legacy of death. He was given headship in relationship to the race, and his sin brought condemnation to all of us. That is not the end of the matter, because the verse continues, "in Christ all will be made alive." Because Christ also represents the race, all who are in Christ will be made alive. The fact that it is not everyone indiscriminately is clear from the next words, "but each in his own turn." That is, *believers* are the "all" who are made alive in Christ. Jesus is the representative head of the entire race of people who are joined to him by faith. There is victory and triumph in the fact that we are not left to condemnation and death. We are instead made to live forever, in Christ.

But the triumph of Christ doesn't end there, because we read that at the end of the age he will hand "over the kingdom to God" (1 Cor. 15:24). He completed all that he was given to do, he accomplished the work of redemption, he delivered his people out of the kingdom of darkness, and he saved them to the uttermost. At the end, the work that was planned in eternity will be given over to God the Father, in complete triumph. Jesus conquered the kingdom of darkness and sat down at the right hand of the Father (Heb. 12:2).

There is no more gratifying word of victory than that found in 1 Corinthians 15:25, "He must reign until he has put all his enemies under his feet." What conquest! This is not a dead, pretend Messiah. This is the conquering King, and the last enemy he will conquer is death. With that conquest, even hell is vanquished for his people.

One of the mottos of the faithful Covenanters in Scotland during the times they were persecuted for their faith was, "he must reign." It was not, "We must make him reign," but "he *must* reign." There is no other option for Christ. He is the King, and the King must reign. One day that reign will accomplish the obliteration of death for his people. The complete triumph of Christ is accomplished for us, and is significant for us, until the end of time.

The significance of the triumph of Christ is seen in the *hope* of the resurrection, for "all will be made alive" (1 Cor. 15:22). The simplest way to state the hope of every true believer in Jesus Christ is with the words "eternal life." This is our hope—that we will live forever. That is what this text assures us when it says, "In Christ, all will be made alive." It gives us hope that as he lives, we too will live. As he conquered death, so we too will conquer death. It sets the tone for all that Paul has to say about the resurrection.

The significance of the triumph of Christ is seen as well, in the *time* of the resurrection. The text says "then the end" (1 Cor. 15:24). This is not about endless discussion, ceaseless debate, whether for the Corinthians or for us today. There comes the time when it is the end. It is hard to imagine, but it will come. Peter, in 2 Peter 3:4, said that the unbelievers ask, "Where is this 'coming' he has promised?" This is how it is, because people cannot even begin to comprehend the end. Most people cannot even begin to comprehend their own end, let alone the end of everything. Peter said about these unbelievers that they deliberately forget about how God caused a flood that destroyed the world. Now "the present heavens and earth are reserved fire, being kept for the day of judgment and destruction of ungodly men." He was saying that when the end takes place, the cosmic destruction against the wicked can be understood only by remembering the flood that wiped out the earth and all the wicked thousands of years ago.

He was also saying that when you trust in Christ and his resurrection, you are getting ready for a certain time. That time is the end. It is not as some who claimed that the end was on January 1, 2000, or any other such date setting. All we know is that one day the world will come to the conclusion of the purpose for which it was created. Then God will destroy the heavens and earth, "but in keeping with his promise we are looking forward to a new heaven and a new earth, the home of righteousness" (2 Peter 3:12–13). As we read, "his kingdom will never end" (Luke 1:33). Neither shall any of Christ's people, those who have trusted savingly in Jesus Christ.

The significance of the triumph of Christ is most obvious in the *comfort* of the resurrection. We read, "The last enemy to be destroyed is death" (1 Cor. 15:26). When people are willing to be honest, they will acknowledge that death is the last great enemy that faces every person. It is the feared and hated final foe of each person, the final foe of all humankind. No one can escape the clutches of death. When you are young, you think that you will never grow old. When you are healthy, you think you will never be sick. When you are breathing, you cannot imagine life not going on. Yet every human being will one day cease to live, for that is the way it is. The young grow old. The healthy become feeble. At some point, even our breath will cease from our bodies, and we will all be dead, if Christ tarries.

But believers are comforted, because we believe that death is destroyed in Christ. We believe that the sting of death is ripped out through Christ. We believe Jesus when he says that if you believe in him, you will live, even if you die (John 11:26). The believer knows that on the other side of death is love and everlasting life for all those who believe. I love the title of the great Puritan author John Owen's treatise on the nature of redemption. He called it "The Death of Death in the Death of Christ." In Christ's death, death was destroyed, and we are assured and comforted in the blessed resurrection of Christ. His resurrection is ours as well. If Christ were dead, then there would be no comfort. When you leave this earth, it is the last time you will hear singing. It is the last glimpse you will ever have of a friend or a loved one. But when Christ rose from the dead, the firstfruits of them that sleep, all things were made new, and we have comfort in his certain triumphant and hope-filled resurrection.

The significance of the triumph of Christ can be appreciated in the *ultimacy* of the resurrection. In Christ's resurrection from the dead and his redemption of his people, he completed the work given to him by the Father. This work now confirms that God is, as it says in 1 Corinthians 15:28, "all in all." When the resurrected Christ delivers up the kingdom to the Father, the last victory will be gained and the kingdom secured for the Father forever. Victory is gained through the destruction of all his enemies. The conquest takes place through the Messiah Jesus, who "must reign until he puts all his enemies under his feet" (1 Cor. 15:25).

Paul clearly understood the centrality of the resurrection. He saw how it is the heart of the Christian faith. He perceived how the church must embrace the Christ, who suffered, died, and rose from the dead. He saw how our comfort and assurance mean something only in connection with a living Christ. He presented that living Jesus to the church, so that throughout all of history God's people would be comforted, strengthened, and blessed. As Christ lives, so too we shall live forever! When we truly trust him, he makes us partakers of that resurrection life. It can't happen by being good. It can't happen by going to church faithfully, but only by surrendering our hearts, minds, and wills to Christ and letting him wash away our sin and guilt, so that we too will live forever in his sight.

**T**he expression "baptism for the dead" raises difficult questions. What did this mean in 1 Corinthians 15:29 when Paul talked about believers being baptized for the dead? He waited until near the end of this astonishing letter to deal with another controversy that was connected with the issue of the resurrection.

There are various understandings of this verse. Dr. Daniel Doriani, a Reformed pastor and adjunct New Testament professor at Covenant Theological Seminary, says of this verse, "The variety of interpretations are so numerous, that we must admit from the outset that no one knows what it means."[1] Even John MacArthur, not known for hesitancy, says of this verse, "as to what this verse does mean, we can only guess, since history has locked it into obscurity."[2] The commentator

---

1. Daniel Doriani, *Tabletalk*, June 1998, 14.
2. John Mac Arthur, *The MacArthur New Testament Commentary, 1 Corinthians* (Chicago: Moody, 1984), 424.

*1 CORINTHIANS 15:29-34*

29Now if there is no resurrection, what will those do who are baptized for the dead? If the dead are not raised at all, why are people baptized for them? 30And as for us, why do we endanger ourselves every hour? 31I die every day—I mean that, brothers—just as surely as I glory over you in Christ Jesus our Lord. 32If I fought wild beasts in Ephesus for merely human reasons, what have I gained? If the dead are not raised,

> Let us eat and drink,
> for tomorrow we die.

33Do not be misled: "Bad company corrupts good character." 34Come back to your senses as you ought, and stop sinning; for there are some who are ignorant of God—I say this to your shame.

Frédéric Godet says, "The diversity of explanations is due, on the one hand, to our ignorance of the usage to which Paul alludes; on the other, to the absence of any parallel expression to guide us in the explanation of it."[3] In the early church, it was Tertullian who said that Paul was talking about baptizing a living Christian in place of one who died without baptism. Epiphanius said that when a nonbaptized adherent died, another member of the church was baptized for his sake, in the

---

3. Frédéric Godet, *Commentary on First Corinthians* (Grand Rapids, Mich.: Kregel, 1977), in loc.

room where the deceased adherent had lived. Then, they thought, the dead individual might escape the penalties of not being baptized. John Chrysostom spoke mockingly of the Marcionites, who concealed a living member under the bed of a dead nonmember. The hidden member would say that he wanted baptism, and they then baptized the dead nonmember in his place. Ambrosiaster implied a certain church ritual when he spoke of the practice that if any one died before receiving baptism, a living person was baptized for him. Chrysostom and Ambrose thought that when anyone had been deprived of baptism by sudden death, the Corinthians were in the habit of substituting a living person for the dead one, to be baptized at his grave.[4]

Heinrici believed that the words of Paul in 1 Corinthians 15:29 were a preliminary argument. He claimed that Paul was rectifying a superstitious custom of the Corinthians and not endorsing or glossing over an unbiblical practice. Theodore Beza believed that it referred to those who bathe the dead prior to burying them. Thomas Aquinas believed it was individuals who were baptized so that they could receive pardon for mortal sins. Hermann Olshausen's interpretation was that these were new converts who were baptized to fill the gap left in the church by Christians who had died. Martin Luther was of the opinion that it was people who were baptized over the graves of the martyrs. John Calvin said, "The words relate to catechumens threatened with death by accident or disease, who ask for baptism, either for their own consolation or for the edification of the brethren."[5] According to Calvin, we are

---

4. John Calvin, *New Testament Commentaries, 1 Corinthians* (Grand Rapids: Eerdmans, 1989), 329.

5. Ibid., 330.

to understand the words "for the dead" in the sense of "in view of death" or specifically "to be soon thought of as dead already."[6] J. B. Lightfoot saw baptism of the dead as not referring to water baptism but to baptism with blood, that is, martyrdom, and referred to the teaching of Christ, who said, "I have a baptism to undergo" (Luke 12:50). The words "for the dead," with this understanding, do not point to the entrance into the church with water baptism but the entrance into the land of the dead through death. These are just a few of the understandings of this unusual reference by the apostle Paul.

While one of the main principles of interpretation is that the plain sense of the text is the most likely rendering, the problem is that no one knows how Paul meant this and how the Corinthians understood it. Even so, it is imperative to understand this verse, because people's eternal souls are at stake in deciding this controversy. The Mormons, with a membership of more than five million souls, base a considerable portion of their view of God on their understanding of this verse. They perform baptisms for dead persons, which they believe save these dead individuals.

Let's start with the immediate context. Paul used the very words about baptism to defend what is at the heart of this chapter, and that is the resurrection of dead believers. Notice what he said: "If there is no resurrection, what will those do who are baptized for the dead?" Paul had heard that some of the Corinthian church denied the bodily resurrection of the dead. The essence of his opening statements in this chapter are summed up in 1 Corinthians 15:12, "How can some of you say that there is no resurrection of the dead?" He then pointed

6. Ibid., 330.

out in verse 13, "If there is no resurrection of the dead, then not even Christ has been raised." He deepened his argument as he made it clear in verse 14 that if Christ has not been raised, then there is no gospel, our faith is useless, and we are still in our sins (v. 17). We are then to be pitied more than anyone on earth (v. 19).

Paul continued his argument by affirming instead that Christ has indeed been raised as the firstfruits of a great resurrection harvest of dead believers, a harvest that will span history from the beginning to the end of the age. This is Paul's final statement on the resurrection of believers in this section. Paul was showing that this practice, whatever it may be, is consistent with belief in the resurrection of the dead. Its significance is clear, as he pointed it out in a rapid-fire succession of examples: "If the dead are not raised, why should I endanger myself every hour?" "If the dead are not raised, why should I risk death every day?" "If the dead are not raised, why should I fight wild beasts?" "If the dead are not raised, it would be better to eat, drink, and be merry, for tomorrow I'm dead" (v. 32).

This is the context, from which there are conclusions. The Corinthians' practice of baptism for the dead must presuppose that there is a resurrection of the dead, which is Paul's main concern. Also, he is not teaching a practice of granting salvation or even the opportunity for salvation, such as the Mormons teach. Whatever is intended in these words, it doesn't mean that people who are dead are saved by this ritual.

Whatever these words mean, Paul did not condemn the action they represented. By this I mean that he never said, "What do you Corinthians think you are doing? Stop this practice immediately!" In other words, Paul's concern was to validate and vindicate the resurrection of the dead, and this practice of the Corinthians, which he mentions in passing, helps him to do so. That's why he used it here in his argument: to show them that the resurrection of the dead is the hope of all believers. If that is the case, I cannot imagine how a baptism for someone who is dead and unbaptized could support the resurrection of the dead. Jesus told the unbaptized thief on the cross that on that very day that he died, he would be in paradise with Jesus. I also cannot understand why such a practice went unchallenged by the apostle if it supported an idea that salvation was in another way than through faith in the Lord Jesus Christ. Therefore, you can understand why I believe that he isn't speaking about water baptism.

The reason there is such confusion among scholars is that they are fixed on that one aspect of baptism—entrance into the visible church. But they have missed another—namely, death. That word *baptism* is used here as a symbol of death. Jesus used it this way in Mark 10:38–39, when he asked James and John, "Can you . . . be baptized with the baptism with which I am baptized?" Since he was speaking of his death, the idea is not that people were baptizing themselves for others who were dead and perhaps unbaptized at their death. But seeing the entirety of the Christian life as a baptism unto death, there is the potential for martyrdom when someone follows Christ. Paul's point is exceedingly simple. There is no sense in giving your life for Christ, which he says he does in 1 Corinthians 15:30–32, and it is stupid to die for the cause of Christ if there is no resurrection. If the dead aren't raised in Christ, then go out and party rather than go out and witness, which could bring suffering to you. Paul, then, was teaching that we enter the same baptism as the martyrs and that what the Corinthian believers were doing was more of a memorial service for the martyrs of the faith than a baptismal service. In these services, they identified themselves with the martyrs in their death and inevitable resurrection!

Paul was saying that if the people of God rejected the reality of the resurrection of the dead, then baptism isn't a life-giving reality but is part of a dead, hopeless church. It becomes a baptism for the benefit of the dead, not the living. It is a baptism for the dead, because all remain dead. It is a pointless gesture, which the context points out. Paul asked what could possibly make his life worth experiencing a baptism of suffering and death if Christ is not raised. He questioned, "Why do I endanger myself every hour? Why do I give myself over to death every day? And I mean that. I really give myself over to that every day. Why did I fight wild beasts at Ephesus?" (I believe the wild beasts of Ephesus are the wild enemies of the gospel he faced while ministering there.) "Why," he asked, "go through this baptism unto death, if there is no resurrection? Why give myself over to death, if there is no resurrection glory? It is all absolutely pointless" (author's paraphrase). As he expressed this thought in 1 Corinthians 15:32, "If the dead are not raised, 'Eat, drink, and be merry, for tomorrow we die.'" This, to me, is the most plausible meaning of this strange expression. Why experience a baptism of death if the church does not rise in glory? If baptism's only concern is for the dead, then what is he calling us to do in giving ourselves for Jesus Christ? It is of no benefit whatsoever. But since the apostle is convinced about the reality of the resurrection of the dead, then giving ourselves to God is what we should all do.

The implications of this verse for our lives are as follows.

Because there is a resurrection of the dead, we should not be afraid to face danger for the sake of Jesus Christ and his gospel. Because there is a resurrection of the dead, we can be bold in facing stiff opposition to the faith. If there was no resurrection, why should anyone in the world face danger in serving Jesus? Why should a Christian go to a dangerous place? Why should we witness to people who might harm us, if indeed there was no resurrection of the dead?

The resurrection of the dead informs us not only how to live in relationship to danger but also how we should live in relationship to pleasure. The idea is that if there is no resurrection of the dead, then a life of pleasure is all that we should desire, because if death is the final end, then pleasure is all there is for this life. But there is a resurrection of the dead. Therefore we should not be addicted to pleasure. Our highest ideal is not to experience pleasure but to experience the approval of God. So we reject some things that might bring us pleasure. You don't eat all you can eat. You don't drink all you can drink. You don't have sexual partners other than your husband or your wife, because you believe that Christ lives, and that by faith in him, you live as well.

If the dead are not raised and people should be concerned only about satisfying their pleasures, then the Corinthians wouldn't have cared about the people around them who were filled with lies and errors. But Paul said that this is deception. "Do not be misled: Bad company corrupts good character." There is probably a broader concern the apostle had: If you believe the teaching of those who deny the resurrection of the dead, you will become a sensualist. Evil company will wind up destroying your character. You will live only for your pleasures, and ultimately this will destroy you. Paul had said that such behavior made sense only if there was no resurrection. But since there is a resurrection, surround yourselves with good teaching and good people who live according to the truth. Make sure that this kind of life is the one you choose for yourself.

Whenever I stay in a hotel, especially in a different time zone, I have to make sure that I am ready to teach on time. I call the switchboard and ask for a wake-up call. Paul does that here for the church. He gives the church a wake-up call! "Wake up to righteousness," he says, for the church had not seen that doctrine was inevitably connected to life. The church had not seen the implications of its rejection of the resurrection of the dead. The church had not seen that such a rejection would lead them into a path of immorality and ultimately destroy them. This is sinful sloth. It is as if you can dreamily let wild and evil teachings and behavior take hold of you, and nothing will happen to you. "Wake up to righteousness," he says, "and stop sinning." He uses a present imperative, which means that if they don't stop sinning, it will become a permanent way of life for them. One commentator said that after plunging into intoxication, they would enter a state of sin, and if they persisted, this state would become permanent. A life so swayed by sin, said this commentator, leads to apostasy. This is how serious the sin of rejecting the resurrection of the dead is to the apostle.

Paul was saying in the strongest possible language that those teaching the church to reject the resurrection of the dead were doing so because they did not know God. They were ignorant. That is why they were rejecting the resurrection. He asked if they wanted to live on the basis of such hideous ignorance. His response concluded this rebuke with the Greek equivalent of "Shame on you!" It is shameful to reject the resurrection. The rejection of the resurrection of the dead is the rejection of the Christian gospel. It is the rejection of Christ, who is alive and reigning at the Father's right hand.

First Corinthians 15:20 says it all: "Christ has indeed been raised from the dead." This is the Christian hope. You are not baptized for the dead. Not at all! Yours is a baptism of the living, for the church of Christ shall rise from the grave to be with Christ and shall reign with Christ. That's why you can face a baptism unto death, because this is not all there is. This life isn't our hope. As Philippians 1:21 says, "To die is gain." Philippians 3:20 says, "Our citizenship is in heaven. And we eagerly await a Savior from there, the Lord Jesus Christ." This is tremendous encouragement for all believers in Jesus Christ. When you trust in Christ, he will, as Philippians 3:21 says, "transform our lowly bodies so that they will be like his glorious body." That is why you can persist in spite of the difficulties, in spite of the doubts, in spite of the troubles, in spite of your weakness, in spite of it all. You can persist, because the living Lord Jesus Christ will save you out of all these things. As he rose from the dead, he will cause you to rise from the dead. "Wake up, people of God." Continue to stand in righteousness. It will all be worth it if you stand firm to the end. Remember, in the resurrection, we know that the best is yet to come. God says that no one who trusts in him will be disappointed. Trust in him and find out. Just wait. You'll see. It will all have been worth it!

# IS THERE MEANING IN LIFE?

I remember sitting through a lecture in the faculty room at the medical center where I was doing a year of post-doctoral study. The thought that hit me was, "This is meaningless. Everything I'm doing here is meaningless." I had obtained all that I had dreamed of attaining. I was on the faculty of a medical center department of psychiatry. I was teaching at the university and was about to begin a private practice in psychotherapy. There seemed to be no limits in view—except for that thought, that unshakeable thought . . . "meaningless." If the psychotherapy work I was doing was meaningless, then everything was meaningless to me. I hadn't yet become a Christian. All I could see was that this was not able to break us free from the bondage that gripped our souls. We were as much dead after years of psychotherapy as we were before it.

I was not the first person, nor would I be the last, to put my hope in my work. Over and over I see individuals whose lives fall apart as they realize that their work cannot define them as persons, let alone save them. During my earliest days

---

**1 CORINTHIANS 15:58**

[58]Therefore, my dear brothers, stand firm. Let nothing move you. Always give yourselves fully to the work of the Lord, because you know that your labor in the Lord is not in vain.

---

treating patients at the hospital connected with the university, I had a fifty-five-year-old patient, who at that time seemed ancient to me. (He was the age I am as I write this book.) He was in intense despair, which I assumed was because of the cancer that was ravaging his life. I was shocked to find out that it wasn't the cancer. His despair was because he had toiled and labored and waited for life—and it never came. This thought produced despair in me as well, because he hadn't given me a cute middle-class neurosis or some terrifying phobia from which I could outspider him. Instead he told me of meaninglessness, and I had no answer for him.

This was my problem. All my efforts to grapple with these issues left me with a sense of meaninglessness. I had tried it all in the 1960s and then had become a doctor of clinical psychology, and my life and my work still seemed meaningless. At about that time, an old poem was turned into what became my favorite song. Listen to a few lines that seemed to sum up my experience:

> I close my eyes, only for a moment and the moment's gone.

> Don't hang on. Nothing lasts forever but the earth and sky.

It slips away and all your money won't another minute
buy.
Dust in the wind. All we are is dust in the wind.
Everything is dust in the wind.

Years passed before I realized that I was gripped by that
song because it was true. Without God, "all we are is dust in
the wind, everything is dust in the wind." Later I was to learn
an additional refrain from Ecclesiastes, "The dust returns to
the ground from which it came." This expresses the terrible reality of death, which hurls us into our sense of meaninglessness. My dilemma was the same as any person who was willing
to honestly think through the issues. It wasn't an accident that
I embraced existentialism as an unbeliever. It was the only option to affirm what I felt in the core of my being, "Meaningless. Everything is meaningless."

The final controversy that Paul addressed in his closing ar-
guments in 1 Corinthians is the issue of meaninglessness. The
Hebrew word for "meaningless" is interesting. It is the word
*hebel,* from which we get Abel, the name of the second son of
Adam. It means "a mere breath." This precious child of Adam
and Eve was given a name that indicated Adam and Eve's post-
fall view of life—a mere breath.

This was the teaching of Moses as well. He wrote Psalm 90 as
an old man of 120 years. Notice what he said in Psalm 90:4–12:

For a thousand years in your sight
    are like a day that has just gone by,
    or like a watch in the night.
You sweep men away in the sleep of death;
    they are like the new grass of the morning—

though in the morning it springs up new,
    by evening it is dry and withered.

We are consumed by your anger
    and terrified by your indignation.
You have set our iniquities before you,
    our secret sins in the light of your presence.
All our days pass away under your wrath;
    we finish our years with a moan.
The length of our days is seventy years—
    or eighty, if we have the strength;
yet their span is but trouble and sorrow,
    for they quickly pass, and we fly away.
Who knows the power of your anger?

For your wrath is as great as the fear that is due you.
    Teach us to number our days aright,
that we may gain a heart of wisdom.

This was also the burden centuries earlier of the preacher of Ecclesiastes. By focusing on work, he touched on what man uses more than anything else to define himself. What he asked was, "If all is meaningless, what gain is there in all your work?" He was asking why anyone should toil in a meaningless universe. He used the phrase "under the sun" twenty-seven times, connected repeatedly to our work. In Ecclesiastes 1:3 he said, "What does man gain from all his labor at which he toils under the sun?" In Ecclesiastes 2:11 he continued, "Everything was meaningless, . . . nothing was gained under the sun." He added a twist in Ecclesiastes 2:17, "So I hated life, because the work that is done under the sun was grievous to me. All of it is meaningless."

In Ecclesiastes 2:18 he reiterated this, "I hated all the things I had toiled for under the sun." In Ecclesiastes 2:20 he wrote, "So my heart began to despair of all my toilsome labor under the sun."

The same idea is presented by David in Psalm 103:15–16, "As for man, his days are like grass, he flourishes like a flower of the field; the wind blows over it and it is gone, and its place remembers it no more." What a bleak picture—a picture of *life without God.* Life under the curse is ultimately meaningless. All that you do, all that you hope, and all the strength and vigor of your youth will soon be over.

The word *meaningless* is used seventy-one times in the Old Testament. Thirty-six of those uses are in Ecclesiastes, where it is found in every chapter except Ecclesiastes 10. This is our human predicament. There is no lasting fulfillment in life. There is no lasting fulfillment in work. There is no lasting fulfillment in love. Even in a best-case scenario, death will finally take these things away from us. Even the *best* life without God is meaningless. The preacher spoke with truth because the world apart from God possesses no meaning in and of itself. But because God lives, *ultimately* the only reality worth expending our lives for is God. Our lives, our work, and our love are all redeemed. What a life we are called to live, where everything we do is meaningful!

This was the concern of Paul. In lives that are redeemed by Christ, we should never slip into the futility of meaninglessness. We should give ourselves to the Lord's work, because he promised that the Lord's work would never, ever be in vain. Instead, just as it is with his Word that never goes out meaninglessly (Isa. 55:10), so too the work of God's children always accomplishes what is intended! Paul said in 1 Corinthians 6:19 that we are the temple of the living God.

Remember the story of Joseph in Genesis. He believed that God sent him the dream in his youth, and Joseph had the audacity to brag about it. This was such an annoyance to his older brothers that while he was obeying his father, bringing food to his brothers, they attempted to thwart the ambitions of their upstart half-brother and sold him into slavery in Egypt. Joseph's superb management of the household of Potiphar led to the adulterous overtures of Potiphar's wife, which Joseph rebuffed. He was thrown into prison when she falsely accused him of attacking her. (Did God see his work? Was this his reward?) While in prison he prophesied the meaning of the dreams of the pharaoh's baker and cupbearer. Urging them to remember him when they were out of prison turned out to be futile, though his predictions came true. (Was God blessing his work?) When the time was right, God called to the mind of the cupbearer that the prisoner Joseph could tell dreams. This was the time that God had appointed Joseph to rise to prominence, particularly so that he could be used to save the lives of God's chosen people by managing the famine preparation in the land of Egypt. Until that time, he had been learning management skills on Potiphar's estate and in prison.

Every situation and every character in this history was crucial to the whole outcome, providentially arranged by God: Joseph's obedience, trust and immaturity as a youth; his hard work and competence as an adult; his father's love and naiveté in favoring him; his brothers' envy; Potiphar hiring him; his wife propositioning him and then falsely accusing him; being sent to the prison; his encounter with Pharaoh's baker and cupbearer, and being forgotten by them, then being remembered later when the king was distressed with his dreams; his brothers coming to Egypt for food. These components were clearly essential *looking back* at the whole, as the writer of this story knew, because he put all these pieces together for us. Because God is sovereign, our work cannot be in vain. Our lives are planned, guided, and blessed by God to accomplish the purposes for which they were created.

The other important thing to remember is that because God lives and sees our work, he will have something to say to us on the judgment day. The Preacher in Ecclesiastes concluded his discussion by saying that we should enjoy God's gifts of work and love in marriage, and remember, "God will bring every deed into judgment, including every hidden thing, whether it is good or evil" (Eccles. 12:14). The apostle Paul, after a long discussion of the resurrection, said, "you know that your labor in the Lord is not in vain." Christ has been resurrected—this is the cornerstone of our faith. Therefore we will be resurrected and we will see God after death. So Paul told us, "Always give yourselves fully to the work of the Lord" (1 Cor. 15:58). Remember he had said in 1 Corinthians 4:5, "Therefore judge nothing before the appointed time; wait till the Lord comes. He will bring to light what is hidden in darkness and will expose the motives of men's hearts. At that time each will receive his praise from God." Later, in his second letter, he wrote, "For we must all appear before the judgment seat of Christ, that each one may receive what is due him for the things done while in the body, whether good or bad" (2 Cor. 5:10).

Knowing these truths, Paul described how we are to live. "Stand firm!" he said. In a world that was devoid of any stability, he told God's people to be settled and firmly situated. We are to be those who will not budge from our commitment to Jesus Christ. This is the same idea that Moses presented to the Israelites when he said, "Do not be afraid. Stand firm and you will see the deliverance the LORD will bring you today" (Exod. 14:13). It is an exhortation that is mentioned again and again in the Scriptures to encourage God's people in times of adversity. The letter ended, "Be on your guard, *stand firm in the faith,* be men of courage, be strong" (1 Cor. 16:13). He opened his second letter to the Corinthians by reminding the people, "Now it is God who makes both us and you stand firm in Christ" (2 Cor. 1:21). Not only must we never be captivated by the lures of a world that sees all as meaningless. We are to stand firm and guard the precious truths of the gospel with our hearts and our lives. How do we *stand firm* in an age of meaninglessness? We remember that Paul said here that we are to be immovable. We Christians are not to be moved from our place, because we are anchored in Christ. Therefore, we are able to overflow in our lives for God, with a labor that is never meaningless.

This word *labor* doesn't mean "hard work" as much as it means "weariness," the weariness that accompanies hard work. It goes back to the idea of a beating, the kind that is administered by taskmasters to slaves. In this context it refers to a wearisome work that is filled with pain and trouble, after which you've accomplished nothing. His words are a call not to give up. Paul's concern was that, "In your labor for the Lord, no matter how difficult, no matter how seemingly discouraging, no matter how wearisome, it will never and can never be without meaning or purpose."

This is why Paul, speaking to those who are in the wearisome battle of life, called them to the right focus when he said, "If you are risen with Christ, seek those things which are above. Set your affection on the things above, not on the things on earth." Christ is risen! This is the heart and soul of the Christian life, as well as being a guarantee of our resurrection. What an antidote to meaninglessness. This whole idea is in connection with the Preacher's message, which urges people to not be seduced by the things that are perishing. These things can only ultimately disappoint. Achievements are left to others when you die, and possessions and pleasures do not satisfy. They prove to be just what the preacher says they are—vanity!

This is why the words of the psalmist resonate in our souls. He cried out to God at those times of inexplicable confusion. He said,

> Show me, O LORD, my life's end
>> and the number of my days;
>> let me know how fleeting is my life.
> You have made my days a mere handbreadth;
>> the span of my years is as nothing before you.
>> Each man's life is but a breath.
>
> Man is a mere phantom as he goes to and fro:
>> He bustles about, but only in vain;
>> he heaps up wealth, not knowing who will get it.
>>> (Ps. 39:4–6)

He didn't want to let life pass in a meaningless blur. He didn't want to get caught up in foolishness and squander his life. He wanted to realize, *while he still had time,* the brevity of life, so that he would use it well. He wanted to "redeem the time because [he knew] the days are evil." He knew that the ordinary passing of days can take on a power all their own. He knew that he could come to make an idol of what he did as easily as making it into nothing. He knew he could forget that he was but a breath. He knew that if he did not come to see himself in a true perspective, he would live only for himself and not for God, and the end of such a life is meaningless.

As we grow in Christ, we come to realize that we are not just "dust in the wind." We know that it is the bitter unbeliever who says, "Everything is dust in the wind." Instead, we understand that our identity is prized. We are "a chosen people, a royal priesthood, a holy nation, a people belonging to God, that you may declare the praises of him who called you out of darkness into his wonderful light" (1 Peter 2:9). This is a wonderful and glorious reality and identity for the people of God.

The meaninglessness of life is smashed in Christ. He is alive. We too will live with him. Our earthly lives are therefore meaningful. Our earthly work is meaningful. When the book is closed on the Corinthian church, it affirms the greatness of God and the victorious life of its saints. They were conquerors even though they came through trial after trial and controversy after controversy. Paul said, "Your work is not in vain in the Lord." Their lives continue to be used by God to teach his people around the world through the centuries. Their lives and their testimony were not one bit in vain. Not in the Lord of glory!

DISCUSSION QUESTIONS

### CHAPTER 1: DIVISIONS IN THE CHURCH
### 1 CORINTHIANS 1:10-17

1. Should the leadership of the church always be in agreement with each other?
2. Why do quarrels arise in the church?
3. What is the solution to the problem of quarrels and divisions in the church?
4. What does Paul mean when he says to "be perfectly united in mind and thought"?
5. What are you to do with people that cause divisions in the church?
6. How is unity to be accomplished in the church?

### CHAPTER 2: THE SCANDAL OF THE CROSS
### 1 CORINTHIANS 1:18-21

1. Why is the preaching of the cross foolishness to those who are perishing?

2. What is the most popular absolute in contemporary philosophy and how does it relate to the gospel?
3. What does it mean to "know nothing except Jesus Christ and him crucified" (1 Cor. 2:2)?
4. What will happen to the wisdom of men?
5. What is the reality that is in connection with God's wisdom?
6. What is the ultimate reality of the "wisdom of God"?

### CHAPTER 3: WERE WE WISE OR FOOLISH?
#### 1 CORINTHIANS 1:26–31

1. Why do people become troublemakers in the church?
2. What does Paul do to address this issue (v. 26)?
3. What is the reminder of Paul (v. 26)?
4. What does the answer to questions 2 and 3 mean?
5. What does it mean when it speaks of your being "called"?
6. What character key is vital in all of this (see Phil. 2:3)?

### CHAPTER 4: WHO IS CHRIST?
#### 1 CORINTHIANS 1:30

1. What does verse 30 say about Christ?
2. What does it mean to be "in Christ Jesus"?
3. What is righteousness?
4. How can we be "found righteous" while not having a righteousness of our own (see Phil. 3:9)?
5. What is sanctification?
6. What is Jesus Christ to *you*?

## CHAPTER 5: JEALOUSY AND QUARRELING
### 1 CORINTHIANS 3:1-9

1. What is the focus of these emerging divisions (v. 3)?
2. What is their problem (v. 3)?
3. What does it mean to be worldly (v. 1)?
4. What can you do to avoid these kinds of problems?
   a. What does the Bible teach about our associations? (Titus 3:10)
   b. What behaviors will guard against such sin? (Gal. 5:22–23)

## CHAPTER 6: CHURCH DISCIPLINE
### 1 CORINTHIANS 5:1-5

1. What kind of sin was worse in the Corinthian church than in the society (v. 1)?
2. What had happened in the Corinthian church (v. 1)?
3. How did the church respond to this sin (v. 2)?
4. What should have been their response (v. 2)?
5. In 1 Thessalonians 4:3 what does sanctification involve?
6. What does a church need to do when there is sin such as this (vv. 3–5)?

## CHAPTER 7: LAWSUITS AGAINST THE CHURCH
### 1 CORINTHIANS 6:1-8

1. What does this passage teach about going to a secular legal establishment to settle a dispute in the church?
2. What does it mean to "appoint as judges even men of little account in the church"(v. 4)?
3. How will the saints judge the world (v. 2)?

4. Why is it so damaging for Christians to have lawsuits against each other (v. 7)?
5. Is there *any* matter over which a believer may go to court with another believer?
6. What should our attitude be toward ourselves in these matters (v. 7)?

## CHAPTER 8: SEXUAL IMMORALITY IN THE CHURCH
### 1 CORINTHIANS 6:12-20

1. What does our culture teach regarding the legitimacy of sexual relations outside of marriage?
2. Does "everything is permissible for me" mean that you can do anything you want?
3. How does sexual immorality deceive (v. 9)?
4. What are the limits of Christian freedom?
5. What is the place of the body on Christian theology (v. 19)?
6. How are young men to treat young women (see 1 Tim. 5:2)?

## CHAPTER 9: MARRIAGE OR CELIBACY
### 1 CORINTHIANS 7:1-7

1. How is marriage described in Genesis 2:18?
2. What must an elder in the church be according to 1 Timothy 3:2?
3. Does this section teach that it is good not to marry?
4. What responsibilities from this passage are involved in having a good marriage?
5. Is Paul teaching celibacy as a higher calling?
6. How does this passage teach that Paul is by no means a chauvinist?

## CHAPTER 10: UNIQUE MARRIAGE SITUATIONS
### 1 CORINTHIANS 7:8–16

1. Why are there so many problems in marriage?
2. Who are those whom Paul calls "unmarried" (v. 8)?
3. What does Paul allow in verse 9?
4. Does verse 10 allow for what we call "legal separations"?
5. What does verse 11 have to say about any unbiblical divorces?
6. Who are "the rest" (v. 12) and what kind of marriages are they in?

## CHAPTER 11: CHRISTIAN LIBERTY
### 1 CORINTHIANS 8

1. Why did eating meats offered to idols cause such trouble in the Corinthian church?
2. What does it mean to be a "strong" or "weak" brother ?
3. What problem does Paul address when he says, "We know that we all possess knowledge"?
4. Since idols are nothing (v. 4), does it matter if you eat meats offered to idols?
5. Does God care about what we eat?
6. How far are we to go to keep our brethren from falling into sin (v. 13)?

## CHAPTER 12: TAINTED BY IDOLATRY
### 1 CORINTHIANS 10

1. What is the overriding concern (v. 14)?
2. Why are the examples of the Israelites mentioned in the early part of the chapter?

3. What is the nature of the warning in verse 12?
4. What significance is involved in idolatry (v. 20)?
5. Ultimately, what is your participation in the Lord's Supper?
6. What blessings come through the Lord's Supper to the believer?

### CHAPTER 13: HEADSHIP IN THE CHURCH
### 1 CORINTHIANS 11:2-16

1. When the apostle speaks of "no other practice in the churches" what practice is in view?
2. Who is intended in Christ's headship over "every man" (v. 3)?
3. To whom are wives to be submissive?
4. What does a husband's headship reflect?
5. What is the significance of the fact that "woman is not independent of man, nor is man independent of woman" (v. 11)?

### CHAPTER 14: TRUE SPIRITUAL BEHAVIOR
### 1 CORINTHIANS 12:1-11

1. Why is the issue of spiritual gifts perhaps the most controversial issue in the church?
2. Should believers try to get spiritual gifts?
3. Why does the apostle remind them of their pagan roots?
4. Does the apostle attack gifts, or something else?
5. How did the Corinthians misuse the gifts?
6. What is the highest gift of the Spirit?

## CHAPTER 15: SPIRITUAL GIFTS
### 1 CORINTHIANS 12:1-11

1. Who is the Person of the Holy Spirit?
2. Why were the gifts given (v. 7; 14:5, 12, Eph. 4:12)?
3. What are the gifts mentioned in this passage?
4. How is wisdom different than knowledge?
5. Is the gift of faith the same as "saving faith"?
6. What passage in the Bible uses all three words for miracle?

## CHAPTER 16: BAPTISM WITH THE HOLY SPIRIT
### 1 CORINTHIANS 12:12-13

1. Who baptizes with the Holy Spirit?
2. What does it mean to be baptized with the Holy Spirit?
3. Who is baptized with the Holy Spirit in Acts 2?
4. What is the main component of a Spirit-baptized life?
5. What is the main purpose of a Spirit-baptized life?
6. What is involved in our witness (Luke 24:45–46)?

## CHAPTER 17: SPEAKING IN TONGUES
### 1 CORINTHIANS 14:1-26

1. On Pentecost day, did the gathering hear understandable or ununderstandable utterances (Acts 2:11)?
2. Are there any occurrences of ununderstandable utterances subsequent to Pentecost day?
3. How do Christians justify a private prayer language that is called "tongues"?
4. What does verse 12 say is the main purpose of the gifts?
5. What is the condemnation of verse 14?
6. What is the essence of the argument about foreigners (v. 21)?

### CHAPTER 18: RESURRECTION OF THE DEAD
### 1 CORINTHIANS 15:20–28

1. What is of first importance in the gospel (vv. 1–11)?
2. "Firstfruits" (v. 20) refers to what?
3. What is the significance of the resurrection of Jesus Christ (v. 22)?
4. When does the resurrection take place (v. 24)?
5. What is the comfort of the resurrection (v. 26)?
6. Through the resurrection of Christ, God is said to be _____ in verse 28.

### CHAPTER 19: BAPTISM FOR THE DEAD
### 1 CORINTHIANS 15:29–34

1. Why is it important to understand the words "baptism for the dead"?
2. What issue is connected with the subject of the baptism for the dead (v. 29)?
3. In what way other than water baptism does Jesus use the term *baptism* (Mark 10:38–39)?
4. How then, does Paul use this expression (vv. 30–32)?
5. What are the implications of this expression?
6. Why are you able to face a baptism unto death?

### CHAPTER 20: IS THERE MEANING IN LIFE?
### 1 CORINTHIANS 15:58

1. What is the meaning of the word "vain"?
2. Why is our work meaningless if it is not "in the Lord"?
3. What are three other references to the meaninglessness of our life and/or work?

4. How do Psalm 103:15–16 and Psalm 90:4–12 help us to deal effectively with the issue of meaninglessness?

5. How are we to "stand firm" (Ex. 14:13; 1 Cor. 16:13; 2 Cor. 1:21) in an age of meaninglessness?

6. What does the word "labor" mean, and what is its significance in this text?

# INDEX OF SCRIPTURE

INDEX OF SCRIPTURE

4:29—133
5—61
5:22—150
5:24—150
5:25—150
5:26–27—89
5:28—150

**Philippians**
1:21—234
2—18
2:2—21
2:3—37
3:9—42
3:20—234
3:21—234

**Colossians**
3:18–19—150

**1 Thessalonians**
4:3—58, 85
4:7—35

**1 Timothy**
3–4—98

3:2—97, 100
3:5—100
3:11—158
3:12—150
4:1–3—99
5:2—86

**2 Timothy**
1:9—35
3:5—50

**Titus**
3:10—49

**Hebrews**
1:1—177, 197
2:3–4—177
2:4—170, 175
5:14—179
12:2—219
12:6—65
12:11—65
12:14—65
13:4—94
13:13—30

**James**
1:15—91
2:2—201
3:13—37
4:1–3—16
4:15—133

**1 Peter**
1:16—36
1:18–19—43
2:9—244
2:11—46
2:23—41
3:1—150
3:7—150
4:10—171
5:5—37

**2 Peter**
1:3—192
3:4—220
3:12–13—221

**1 John**
1:9—87
4:11—133

259

**Dr. Richard L. Ganz** is the senior pastor of a growing church in Ottawa, Canada. He is also president of Ottawa Theological Hall, where he teaches biblical counseling. He lectures at universities, seminaries, and churches and does numerous conferences internationally.

Dr. Ganz was born in New York City and raised in a Jewish home. He graduated from the City University of New York with a psychology degree, then went on to earn his Doctorate in Clinical Psychology at Wayne State University.

Dr. Ganz practiced clinical psychology and taught at Syracuse University and the Upstate Medical Center complex before coming to faith in Jesus Christ. He then attended Westminster Theological Seminary where he earned his Master of Divinity degree, and worked at the Christian Counseling and Educational Foundation, with Dr. Jay E. Adams. Dr. Ganz is the author of several books including *Psychobabble, The Secret of Self-Control,* and *Free Indeed.* He and his wife Nancy have four daughters and live on a farm in the Ottawa valley.

Breaking Free! is the counseling ministry of Dr. Richard L. Ganz. If you are interested in a Breaking Free! seminar (or other biblical counseling seminars) for your local churches, you can e-mail Dr. Ganz at: richganz@storm.ca